Cover: Eduard J. F. Bendemann *Wilhelm von Schadow on his Sickbed* 1860 (detail)

The Düsseldorf Academy

and the Americans

An exhibition of drawings and watercolors

organized by
The High Museum of Art
Atlanta, Georgia

Published by The High Museum of Art, Atlanta, Georgia
Library of Congress Catalogue Card No. 72–83953

Designed by Graham Johnson/Lund Humphries
Printed in Great Britain by Lund Humphries

Contents

The Düsseldorf Academy and the Americans

The exhibition will be seen at the following museums:

Munson–Williams–Proctor Institute
Utica, New York
January 7-February 11, 1973

National Collection of Fine Arts
Smithsonian Institution
Washington, D.C.
April 27-July 28, 1973

The High Museum of Art
Atlanta, Georgia
September 23-October 28 1973

This project is supported by a grant from the
National Endowment for the Arts in Washington, D.C., a Federal agency.

Lenders to the Exhibition

Kunstmuseum, Düsseldorf, Germany.

Addison Gallery of American Art, Phillips Academy,
Andover, Massachusetts.

The Baltimore Museum of Art, Baltimore, Maryland.

Cincinnati Art Museum, Cincinnati, Ohio.

Cooper-Hewitt Museum of Decorative Arts and Design,
Smithsonian Institution, New York, New York.

Corcoran Gallery of Art, Washington, D.C.

William Hayes Fogg Art Museum,
Harvard University, Cambridge, Massachusetts.

Dr. William H. Gerdts, New York, New York.

Mr. and Mrs. Maurice Glickman, New York, New York.

The High Museum of Art, Atlanta, Georgia.

Hirschl & Adler Galleries, Inc., New York, New York.

Kennedy Galleries, New York, New York.

Florence Lewison Gallery, New York, New York.

The Library of Congress, Washington, D.C.

Mrs. Catherine Maynard, Atlanta, Georgia.

The Metropolitan Museum of Art, New York, New York.

Museum of Fine Arts, Boston, Massachusetts.

Free Library of Philadelphia, Philadelphia, Pennsylvania.

St. Louis Mercantile Library Association, St. Louis, Missouri.

Mr. and Mrs. Ralph Spencer, New York, New York.

Mr. Kurt Versen, Deerfield Beach, Florida.

Mr. and Mrs. Gudmund Vigtel.

Mr. William Woodville, VIII, Washington, D.C.

Foreword

The history of American art has been investigated extensively over the past several decades, both in general surveys and in monographs, and while specific American characteristics have been uncovered by these studies, it has also become evident that the influence from Europe pervaded almost everything produced by the American artists of the eighteenth and nineteenth centuries.

As often as not, American art before the Civil War has been seen as an off-shoot of the English tradition, although art historians have begun to explore the influences of the Dutch, of the Claudian landscape tradition, and the stormy romanticism of Italian painters such as Salvator Rosa. Neo-Classicism, Barbizon lyricism and the academic attitudes of the Salon painters Couture and Gerôme were also undeniable elements in American painting of the last century.

While the role of the Düsseldorf Academy in American painting between the 1840's and the 1860's is a matter of record, no museum has, to our knowledge, undertaken a systematic comparison between the work of the Academy professors and their American pupils. Düsseldorf qualities were prevalent in mid-century American painting, not only because several of our best artists studied there, but also because the gloss and sentiment so characteristic of the Academy style suited mid-century tastes to perfection. However, post-Civil War attitudes, combined with a new pre-occupation with painterly realism emanating from the master studios in Munich and Paris, made the earlier theatrics seem irrelevant, and the Düsseldorf manner became hopelessly outmoded during the last decades of the nineteenth century.

We organized this exhibition to demonstrate the effects of the Düsseldorf Academy on American art through an examination of the drawings and watercolors by the principal American painters who studied at the Academy and by their teachers. The logical person to select the works and write the essay for our catalogue was Donelson F. Hoopes who had prepared another study on American art for us only two years ago – his review of nineteenth-century American landscape painting for our exhibition, *The Beckoning Land*. When he was Curator of Paintings at The Brooklyn Museum, he organized with Axel von Saldern an exhibition in 1967, *The Triumph of Realism*, a study of the influence of the Munich and Paris schools on American painting in the third quarter of the nineteenth century. Our thanks for his most valued collaboration are again due Mr. Hoopes, who since the completion of this project has been appointed Curator of American Art of the Los Angeles County Museum of Art.

This exhibition is the direct result of a tour in the spring of 1970 of the German museums which I undertook with sponsorship from *Inter Nationes*. A visit to the Düsseldorf Museum produced a useful meeting there with officials who encouraged me to request loans from the Museum's very extensive holdings of Academy drawings, and the idea to use this chance to investigate the relationship between the nineteenth century professors and their American pupils followed closely. The collaboration of the Düsseldorf Museum became a key to our exhibition, and I would like to use this opportunity to thank the Museum's Director, Dr. Wend von Kalnein, who made these loans possible through his personal interest and supervision, and also for his very informative essay on the Academy. Dr. Dieter Graf of the Museum's staff has been especially helpful in providing us with information on the German loans. Our gratitude is extended to all lenders to this exhibition who so generously allowed us to draw on their collections for our exhibition.

The exhibition is a truly international undertaking, not only through the collaboration of German and American museums, but also because the project enjoys the financial support of the German government as well as that of our National Endowment for the Arts. We are deeply grateful to His Excellency, Ambassador Rolf Pauls, and to Consul General Roland H. A. Gottlieb, for their keen interest, and to the Endowment's Chairman, Nancy Hanks.

I must also record here my appreciation for the confidence shown to the High Museum by the Directors of the Munson-Williams-Proctor Institute and the National Collection of Fine Arts, Edward H. Dwight and Joshua Taylor, who agreed to present this exhibition in their respective museums as part of their program of American studies.

Untold hours of hard work go into efforts such as this, and the inevitable times of crisis which tested the staff's fortitude demand my most sincere expressions of thanks, especially to my assistant, Susan Butler, and to Connie Jesse, the Museum's Registrar. Their support and their keen participation in these labors were indispensable.

Gudmund Vigtel, Director
The High Museum of Art

Acknowledgements

The assistance of many helpful persons made the organization of this exhibition possible. Among those who generously offered their knowledge and interest to this exhibition a large debt of gratitude goes to: Edward H. Dwight, Museum of Art, Munson-Williams-Proctor Institute, Utica; Stuart P. Feld and Cecily Langdale, Hirschl & Adler Galleries, New York; Barbara Groseclose, Chicago; Dr. Francis S. Grubar, The George Washington University, Washington, D.C.; Gordon Hendricks, New York; Patricia Hills, The Whitney Museum of American Art, New York; Marilyn Friedman Hoffman, Brockton Art Center, Brockton, Massachusetts; Dr. Wend von Kalnein, the Museum of Art, Düsseldorf; Vera Leuschner, Göttingen; Florence Lewison, New York; Dr. E. P. Richardson, Philadelphia; Dr. Ernst Scheyer, Detroit; Wendy J. Shadwell, New York; George Schriever, M. Knoedler & Company, New York. John Davis Hatch, Lenox, Massachusetts; Kurt Versen, Tenafly, New Jersey; and William Woodville VIII, Washington, D.C., all provided valuable information concerning the loans to the exhibition.

The greater number of works included in the exhibition come from public collections and for their help we especially thank Richard J. Boyle and Carolyn R. Shine, Cincinnati Art Museum; Charles E. Buckley and Alexandra Bellos, The St. Louis Art Museum; William G. Pettus, Jr., St. Louis Mercantile Library Association; Dr Alan Fern and Herbert J. Sanborn of The Library of Congress; Linda Boyer Gillies and Natalie Spassky, The Metropolitan Museum of Art, New York; Robert F. Looney, The Free Library of Philadelphia; Dorothy Phillips and Martha Morris, Corcoran Gallery of Art, Washington; Mrs. Elliott E. Topkins, Eleanor Sayre, Linda Thomas, and Stephanie Loeb, Museum of Fine Arts, Boston; and William Truettner, National Collection of Fine Arts, Washington, D.C.

Donelson F. Hoopes

The Düsseldorf Academy

Wend Von Kalnein
Director, Museum of Art, Düsseldorf

The Düsseldorf Academy was one of the most fertile of German art schools and certainly the most important among those institutions in Germany during the first half of the nineteenth century. Its artists strode from success to success, admired by the public, celebrated by the critics, and counting the church, the nobility, and the middle class among their patrons. The school of Düsseldorf was a magic word which opened all doors and evoked notions among contemporaries of painstaking technique and significant content. Its influence stretched over all of Germany and, through the numerous pupils from abroad, far beyond its borders, especially in Scandinavia and North America. It was not until the schools in Munich and Berlin gained in power during the last half of the century that the Academy lost its lustre.

The Düsseldorf Academy was based on an illustrious tradition. An "Academy of Painting, Sculpture and Architecture" had been founded in the name of the Electors Palatine in the city in 1773, under the leadership of the director of the Electoral Art Gallery, one of the largest and most beautiful collections of its time. This union had proven itself most useful over a period of more than thirty years not only insofar as the two institutions were concerned, but also for the reputation of Düsseldorf, which was a small capital at that time, ruled by a governor. The union was torn violently apart when Düsseldorf became Prussian in 1805, and shortly thereafter French. The Art Gallery was moved to Munich where the Electors Palatine had gained the succession to the Bavarian Dukes, and the union was never again restored because the Rhineland, including Düsseldorf, finally became Prussian at the conclusion of the Napoleonic Wars. The Art Gallery remained in Munich as a Palatinate family possession, while the Academy was reopened in 1819 by the Prussian government and joined with what was left in Düsseldorf of the official art collections.

This new effort had a slow beginning. The new Director, Peter von Cornelius, approached his task in a half-hearted way. He had accepted a commission from the King of Bavaria to decorate the "Glyptothek" with frescoes. He taught in Düsseldorf only during the winter and worked in Munich with his pupils during the summer. Peter von Cornelius finally left Düsseldorf once and for all in May of 1825, after he had been appointed director of the Munich Academy. Most of his older students went with him.

It was only after this interlude that Düsseldorf experienced its most brilliant period. Wilhelm Schadow arrived in Düsseldorf in 1826 when he was 38, and took over the directorship after Cornelius. With a stroke a new era had begun.

Schadow, who differed totally from his predecessor, struck out into new directions rather than continuing Cornelius's work. Unlike Cornelius, who was a native of Düsseldorf, the new director came from Berlin, the son of the famous sculptor Gottfried Schadow. He had spent a long time in Rome and lived for nine years with Overbeck and the other Nazarenes, and had joined them in their spiritual attitudes. Nevertheless, he differed from his friends in many ways. He was closer to nature and had a very direct feeling for color. It was his opinion that even "the ideal subject should be imbued with palpable life, and that its representation would remain an incomplete work of art without the basis of natural reality." Where Schadow differed particularly from Cornelius was in his preference for easel painting over fresco. Only oil painting was, in his view, capable of dealing with the opulence of the visual world.

Added to this, Schadow showed considerably greater ability as a teacher than had Cornelius. This ability enabled him to establish close relationships with his students already in Berlin, and induced a large number of his pupils to follow him when he moved to Düsseldorf, a factor which gave the Academy much needed new blood. After Cornelius had left, only a few students remained. Among those, only one, Schirmer, was of artistic importance. With Schadow, however, came, among others, Lessing, Hildebrandt, Hübner, Bendemann, Carl Sohn—names which were to justify the reputation of the Düsseldorf School. These Prussian painters, none of whom was more than twenty-one, brought the late romanticism of the Berlin School to Düsseldorf where the style of the "German Romans" and the French school of David had held sway—in the person of Heinrich Christoph Kolbe. Medieval castles, warrior monks, legend, and history made their entry.

Schadow searched for the "meaningful ideas" for his pictures among religious history painting and among ideal themes—as had Cornelius. The contradictions between idealism and naturalism dominate Schadow's work, however. The naturalistic detail becomes so insistent that it destroys the unity and mood of his religious pictures (the predominant theme of his work), pictures painted in numerous churches which we find difficult to endure because of their mawkish sentimentality.

In contrast to Cornelius, Schadow possessed, above all, extraordinary talents as an administrator. It is for this reason that he was able to create the foundation for success in the form of his reorganization of the Academy, the basis for his reputation even today. As a preliminary to the actual studies, he established a two-year course and the preparatory classes where studies from the model and drawings from plaster casts as well as copying were to be augmented by portrait studies. Only those who had proven themselves in portraiture were allowed to paint the figure. The introduction of master classes was another important innovation. The master pupils who were assigned their own studios and worked in close contact with their teachers, were more than mere assistant teachers at the Academy. They contributed to the characteristics of style in the Schadow tradition through their own close interrelationships. The Düsseldorf Academy owed its high level of portraiture and its popularity among contemporaries to this thorough training and the continued studies of nature.

Schadow's tolerance in artistic matters and his ability to recognize individual talent also played an important role. Thus the establishment of a landscape class at the Academy in 1839 under Schirmer's leadership opened the road to the development of landscape painting, marked by such names as Schirmer, Pose, Achenbach, and others. Schirmer was among the most important teachers of the Academy. He was influenced by Lessing with whom he had already founded an "Association for Landscape Composition" in 1827 and he managed to free himself of all fetters of late romanticism with an intensive study of nature which had taken him to the Eifel Mountains since 1829, and later to Switzerland, Normandy, and Italy. He

Figure 1 Andreas Achenbach (German, 1815–1910), *The Old Academy in Düsseldorf*, 1831, oil on canvas, h. 25¼″ × 31⅞″, Collection of the Museum of Art, Düsseldorf, Germany.

arrived at a modern, realistic structure in his loosely painted landscape studies where the eye is led into the distance without any foreground props. Nearly all of the Düsseldorf landscape painters were the products of his classes; among others, Pose, Lasinsky, Becker and Caspar Scheuren.

Most famous of all, however, was Andreas Achenbach, one of the most gifted landscape artists of the century. The view from his window of the old Academy (Figure 1) which he had already painted in 1831 at the age of 16, must be regarded as a pioneer work in its closely observed realism. Nothing is left here of Lessing's late romanticism which was so evident at first among all the others. Andreas Achenbach became the strongest exponent of the Dutch landscape, an influence toward which the Düsseldorfers turned during the 1840's. Both of the Achenbach brothers, Andreas and the much younger Oswald, personified Düsseldorf landscape painting even beyond the turn of the century when their styles had already stiffened into a routine.

Genre painting, which also prepared the ground for realism, developed simultaneously with Schadow's silent acquiescence. Schrödter, Hasenclever and the Preyer brothers were the leading spirits in this field. Schrödter was the first to use everyday themes and to caricature the sentimental-ideal direction of the Academy through sarcastic humor. Hasenclever, who was influenced by English tastes and politically involved, showed the middle class with direct freshness and ridiculed the tearful contemporary literature with his *Jobsiade*.* Both were among the founders of realism in Düsseldorf and among those who championed a new social and politically oriented order, something which Schadow never forgave them and which was to lead to a break with the Academy. A picture such as Hasenclever's *Studio Scene* of 1836 predicts Menzel in this context.

However, the great popularity of the Schadow school lay principally in other areas—in wall decoration and in paintings of romantic and poetic bent. Cornelius had given the School renewed interest in fresco painting which had fallen into disuse since medieval times. The decoration of the garden room of Heltorf Palace near Angermund became the first major commission for the School. Stürmer, a pupil of Cornelius, had already begun a series here on the life of Frederic Barbarossa. The project was completed during 1829–1838 by the Schadow pupils, Mücke, Lessing, and Plüddemann. Their work, next to Stürmer's contribution, underscored the unfavorable aspects of fresco as compared to the deep tonalities of oil painting. Other commissions followed which brought fame and honors to the School—decorations in the City Hall of Elberfeld, in the Hall of Knights and the Chapel of Stolzenfels Palace near Koblenz, and in the Apollinaris Church of Remagen. The latter was the principal work of the group of Nazarenes consisting of Deger, Ittenbach, and the brothers Karl and Andreas Müller, artists who had gathered around Schadow after his visit to Rome in 1830. The languishing sentimentality which permeated this work was criticized even then.

The leaders of the romantic-poetic style were Lessing, Bendemann, Hildebrandt, and Sohn. It was essentially the result of their art which contributed to the popularity of the Düsseldorf School. Bendemann's *Grieving Jews* (Wallraf-Richartz Museum, Cologne), Lessing's *Royal Couple in Mourning* (Hermitage, Leningrad), Hildebrandt's *The Murder of King Edward's Sons*, Sohn's *Tasso and the Two Leonores* (both in the Kunstmuseum, Düsseldorf) and others, were highly prized works which, according to contemporary criticism introduced a new era. The romantic-elegaic mood which penetrated all of these pictures as well as the escape into the past and into poetry matched popular tastes perfectly. The lifelike rendering was felt to be an expression of artistic perfection and the discernible historicism was accepted as a "clear mirror of the times." Gottfried Schadow wrote at the time that "the products of the Düsseldorf Academy in the Berlin exhibitions surpassed all works from other places, or even from Italy." Immermann, an impartial witness and observer, wrote in his *Düsseldorfer Beginnings*: "The forces at the School have unmistakably produced a national mood through color and form, a mood from which the School is only beginning to disassociate itself in a conscious way. And if this frame of mind is specifically of the sentimental-romantic variety, and if the soft, the distant, the musical and the contemplative predominates rather than the palpable, the forceful, the real, the active, why then must you change the painting when you praise poetry to which you all owe some of your background?"

---

*Illustrations for an eighteenth century parody of heroic epics entitled *The Life, Opinion and Deeds of Hieronymus Jobs* by K. A. Kortum.

The champions of the secular romantic-poetic direction, particularly Hildebrandt and Sohn, owed their inspirations specifically to poetry. They were the outcome of the literary influences which were offered to the young painters in Schadow's home, and of the evenings of readings which took place there when Justice von Uechtritz presented classical works as well as his own. Their influences were above all to be found in the theatre. Immermann was the decisive figure here. He brought the painters into contact with the works of Goethe and Shakespeare, the poems of Uhland, the epics of Ariosto and Tasso. The artists participated on the stage themselves, either in the preparations for official performances or with their own plays, and they found here their decisive influences. The super-realism of the Düsseldorf style cannot be understood without the study of contemporary stage properties, and the shallow foreground of the paintings where the action takes place is directly related to the uncluttered front of the stage where the theatrical *tableau vivant* was placed, a technique suggested by Tieck and realized by Immermann in Düsseldorf. This close connection with the stage produced a theatrical quality in Düsseldorf painting which clearly distinguished it from the style of Munich or Berlin and which did not prove to be to its advantage, especially in later genre painting.

The golden age of the Düsseldorf Academy took place between 1826 and ca. 1860. And yet there was friction even in the 1830's between the Rhinelanders at the Academy and the Prussians who had arrived with Schadow, leading, among other things, to the departure for Frankfurt of the young Rethel, one of the most gifted of the Düsseldorfers. A free association of artists developed outside the Academy, in conscious opposition to the circle around Schadow, a group of artists who reproached the Academy director for his biased preference of history painting and his disdain of profane art. There were, in addition, the political and social tensions of the period before the Revolution of 1848 in which the artists took an active part. Proof of this are the critical and socially involved pictures by Hübner, Schwingen and Hasenclever, as well as Andreas Achenbach's caricatures. The establishment in 1848 of the artists' association, "Malkasten" ("Paint Box"), which also included academy students, became the final expression of liberal anti-Prussian currents. However, the "Malkasten" also turned out to be a cohesive force. The cameraderie of this club, which found its climax in the famous celebrations, was no small contribution to the unity of the Düsseldorf Academy.

The romantic influence waned gradually after the Revolution of 1848, and while Düsseldorf portraiture found its zenith in the work of Knaus and Leutze, romantic painting began to decline. The natural was being replaced by the academic and the old guard began to disperse after mid-century. Schirmer left Düsseldorf in 1854 in order to assume the leadership of the art school at Karlsruhe, to be followed by Lessing and Schroedter a few years later. Hildebrandt retired in 1854, a year after Hasenclever had died. Schadow himself was forced to give up his leadership of the Academy in 1859 due to serious illness. His brother-in-law and successor, Bendemann, was not capable of giving the School a renewed stability and he, himself, resigned in 1867. The point of gravity was thus moved to the group of artists who had remained outside the Academy. The last great representatives of Düsseldorf painting were Andreas Achenbach, Knaus, and Vautier, the champions of landscape, portraiture and genre respectively, while the history painters fell into a hopelessly rigid routine.

The spiritual and political currents of the time were faithfully reflected by the Düsseldorf

Academy. It fed on the spirit of Schadow and failed as his reputation and fame waned. Düsseldorf became just another art center with its Academy living on past glories, as Berlin moved toward center stage during the 1870's and became, with Munich, the artistic capital of Germany. But it was only the twentieth century which managed to counter the world of Schadow with a new world.

The Düsseldorf Academy and the Americans

by Donelson F. Hoopes

Curator of American Art, Los Angeles County Museum of Art

In 1841, Emanuel Leutze, the first important American artist to work in Düsseldorf, made his appearance in that city. The importance of Leutze's position there during the two decades that followed cannot be overstated, with respect to the awakening of attention in America to this German art center. With the establishment of the quasi-commercial Düsseldorf Gallery in New York in 1849, the primacy of the Düsseldorf school of painting, with its close bonds to the Academy, became firmly established in America as a model for a significant number of other American artists. Thus, for a brief period lasting until 1860, the name of Düsseldorf became the epitome of all that Americans thought admirable in the realm of painting. Ironically, at the very moment of its triumph in America, that very species of sentimental genre painting which the Germans call *Düsseldorfisch*, had fallen out of favor in Europe. The shift began gradually toward a school of realism in art whose capital became Munich. By the 1870's American realist painters like Frank Duveneck and William Merritt Chase had become disciples of Wilhelm Leibl. At the same time Paris was emerging as the dominant art capital of Europe under the leadership of these realists Gustave Courbet and Edouard Manet.

William Morris Hunt was not only one of the earliest Americans to encounter the Düsseldorf Academy but was also most prophetic in his evaluation of the qualities upon which the school prided itself. In the early 1840's Hunt briefly sampled the routine of the Academy before going on to Paris and the studio of Thomas Couture. He quickly decided against the Academy on the grounds that he could not commit his career to "the principle that the education of art genius, of a mechanic and of a student of science were one and the same thing – a grinding, methodical process for the accumulating of a required skill." Hunt's temperament, romantic that he was, required much more than was deemed necessary in art by those German teachers in Düsseldorf who were the inheritors of the cool emotion and the hard, dry style of painting – a style handed down from that peculiarly monastic order of German artists, the *Lukasbund*, commonly known as the Nazarenes.

The Nazarenes, a group of German and Austrian artists whose number included Johann Overbeck, Philipp Veit, and Peter von Cornelius, was founded in Vienna around 1810 as a consequence of the awakening of the Romantic impulse in European culture. The Nazarenes turned to the Bible as a source of inspiration for their art. Furthermore, they were looking to their own cultural heritage, specifically to the art of the Middle Ages in Germany. When they took up residence in Rome in an abandoned monastery around the year 1810 their objective was to fuse their interests and to enrich their interpretations through a concerted study of the Italian *quattrocento*. They totally rejected the rigid studio atmosphere then prevailing in European academies of art, and strove to create an atmosphere of comradely association between teacher and pupil. During the period of the Napoleonic Empire, the Electors of the

Neuberg-Palatinate who had made Düsseldorf a center of the arts, moved their court to Munich, and with the court went most of the collections of paintings. The art school experienced a similar decline, which continued until the Council of Vienna in 1815. Düsseldorf was thereafter ruled by Berlin, and appointments to fill the vacancies at the Düsseldorf Academy quickly determined its subsequent character. The "fervent and austere" Cornelius, as he was called, assumed the directorship of the Academy in 1819 and set about the following year to reorganize the institution.

Henceforth, the Academy was to be divided into three sections: elementary drawing in geometry and perspective; drawing from the "antique" as well as from the live model with *some* painting permitted; and, advanced students were permitted to work on their own compositions in co-operation with the master. While this last condition was simply a restoration of the Nazarene teacher-pupil relationship, and could only be the logical consequence of Cornelius's hand at the helm, it was the provision for intermediate students to be allowed to use color that proved innovative. Cornelius stated his aims clearly: there was to be "no choking and intimidating of the spirit"; every student was to keep his "natural, unaffected, freely developed peculiarity and independence." He was a better theorist than administrator, and by 1826 Berlin replaced him with the younger Wilhelm Schadow, who amplified the teaching provisions at Düsseldorf by introducing the "master class" concept: advanced students were to participate in the master's own work. Schadow had been with the Nazarenes in Rome, and many of his teaching ideas stemmed from that experience; however, later in Berlin, he was associated with the painter Wilhelm Wach, who had been a student of David and Gros in Paris. Wach introduced Schadow to the tutorial method of the David and Gros studios. But Schadow's most important contribution was his effective choice of a faculty to assist him. Most of them had been former students at Berlin; they comprised an academy in their own right: Heinrich Mücke, anatomical drawing; Carl F. Sohn, figure drawing; Theodore Hildebrandt, portraiture; Carl Lessing, historical painting. To this group he added in 1831, a landscape painter, Johann Schirmer, whose ideal Italianate pictures coincided nicely with Schadow's preconceptions of formality and monumentality. Even though Schadow's own canon of ideal form was succumbing, perhaps unconsciously, to Biedermeier taste, as evidenced in his drawings for allegories of comedy and tragedy (Figures 57, 58) he still ruled the Academy as an autocrat whose staunch Catholicism insisted on the primacy of historical and religious subject matter. Yet, by admitting Schirmer to the faculty, Schadow had set the doors of the Academy ajar, for at the heart of landscape painting lay the germ of realism around which a generation of young artists would gather. The influx of this new talent immediately imparted to the Academy's curriculum vigorous departments of history, landscape and genre painting. These new men also helped to change the emphasis from religious to secular subject matter. In particular, Lessing, an ardent Protestant, was the leader in removing the last vestiges of Cornelius's Catholic-Nazarene domination which had been for so many years the guiding force of the Academy.

Thus, by the time of Leutze's arrival in Düsseldorf in 1841, the Academy had become a thoroughly liberal institution; instruction in elementary drawing, geometry, and perspective was kept at a minimum for the benefit of new students, but the emphasis lay squarely upon independent achievement. The most talented students were chosen by Schadow for his

Meisterklasse and they received private studio space in the Academy building. Exceptional talent became the means for achieving a level of status within the Academy and insured such special talents a position of near-equality with the resident instructors. Moreover, the instructors themselves were encouraged by the administration to accept private pupils, thereby eliminating any direct control over certain new arrivals by the Academy. It was precisely into this situation that Leutze was precipitated. He was accepted immediately by Lessing as a private pupil and during his first weeks in the studio produced a historical subject, *Columbus before the Council of Salamanca.*

Leutze, who was born in Gmünd and brought to America as a child, found the orientation to German art a natural consequence of his birthright. In his youth Leutze had already demonstrated a remarkable talent, and at 21 he had been commissioned to paint portraits of a number of prominent government figures for inclusion in a portrait collection then being formed in Washington, D.C. Through the influence of a Philadelphia patron, Edward L. Carey, Leutze was able to acquire the necessary funds for his European education. He apparently had no hesitation in choosing Düsseldorf. In a letter home he wrote: "When I arrived here, I was happy to be immediately admitted by the best society and soon was showered with evidences of friendship . . . I have already achieved my goal and, once having won a name in Europe as an artist, I need have no fear in America."

Leutze perhaps was unsuited by temperament to follow the example of the Düsseldorf manner where the Academy favored laborious preparations for the execution of a painting of meticulous finish. He preferred a more rapid approach which lacked minuteness of detail. This tendency inspired him to look elsewhere for a time; in 1842 he went to Munich to study the works of Kaulbach whose style was more sweeping and dramatic than that of Lessing. His absence from Düsseldorf continued through nearly three years during which time he visited Venice and Rome in search of the grand style of Italian Renaissance painting. During the next years Leutze concentrated upon subjects taken from important incidents in English history as well as subjects relating to the discovery and early settlement of America. In the self-caricature (Figure 126) Leutze gives us an insight about his prodigious outpouring during these years. He works at an ambitious composition while dreaming of America represented by the Capitol building and an ear of corn—images swimming in a phantasma of free associations.

From the evidence of his early drawings, Leutze's energies were expended in conscious emulation of a variety of styles; his 1841 pencil composition of a group of children at play (Figure 127) reveals a possible awareness on his part for the work of Philipp Otto Runge (1777–1810), and his *Cathedral Ruins* (Figure 117) from about 1845 bears strong hints of the influence of Andreas Achenbach, particularly in subject matter and treatment as seen in the latter's *Gothic Church Ruins* (Figure 11) from about 1831. This romantic subject matter also appears in drawings within the present exhibition such as in the examples by Caspar Scheuren (Figures 59, 60). While the latter tends to be objective in his treatment of the subject matter, Leutze apparently fell under the influence of the more ideal and generalized treatments of the Nazarene type of landscape as can be found in the work of Schulten.

Carl Lessing's studio became the gathering place for most of the young Americans who came to Düsseldorf in the 1840's. Lessing, himself, had arrived in the city in 1826 when he became

Figure 11 Andreas Achenbach
(German, 1815–1910), *Gothic Church Ruins*,
1831, oil on canvas, h. $9\frac{7}{8}''$ × w. $7\frac{1}{2}''$,
Collection of the Museum of Art,
Düsseldorf, Germany.

a teacher under Schadow. His drawing, *Mountain Landscape in a Storm* (Figure 31), reveals his early predisposition to the northern German Romanticism and to its chief exponent, Caspar David Freidrich; however, he was not the only one of the Düsseldorf artists to inject that strain of Romanticism into the diversity of points of view that made for the stylistic complexity of the Düsseldorf School. Andreas Achenbach, who had traveled extensively in Northern Europe before coming to the Düsseldorf Academy in 1835, shows his almost total reliance upon Friedrich's mysticism in a watercolor like *Forest Deep in Snow* (Figure 3). These two artists represent the continuation of the Cornelius-Schadow establishment on one hand and the independent group of artists who lived in Düsseldorf but who were not allied with the Academy on the other. In a number of drawings dating from the early 1830's (see Figures 32, 33, 34) Lessing proclaimed the essence of the official Academy style. In spite of the meticulous drawing and the apparent seriousness of his purpose, Lessing's conception of medieval romance and war is unconvincing, especially when compared with the work of his contemporary, Eugène Delacroix.

The significant fault of the Düsseldorf historical style lay in the seeming inability of its artists to inject a feeling of spontaneity in such small, highly finished studies, much less in the finished paintings. Lessing's style, especially, as seen in his ambitious historical compositions exemplifies a characteristic Düsseldorf approach to the handling of dramatic themes. His work in this vein is typical of the Düsseldorf *tableau* style, which was to represent action in almost any given subject as a moment frozen in time. Furthermore, the actors in the Düsseldorf *tableau* seem enclosed within the context of a shallow proscenium. Each event becomes completely isolated within the borders of a given composition. This condition becomes even more noticeably artificial as the subject matter grows more grandoise. This static quality inherent in the Düsseldorf approach tends to destroy the vitality latent in such dramatic themes as Lessing's *The Crusaders Find a Spring in the Desert* (Figure 37). It is interesting to note that the latter drawing was created the same year that Leutze had established a preliminary drawing for his *Washington Crossing the Delaware* (Figure 125). Worthington Whittredge, who came to Düsseldorf that year noted in his *Autobiography*: "I had not been in Düsseldorf an hour before he showed me a pencil sketch of this subject . . . This little sketch was substantially the same in its arrangement as the completed picture." Leutze relied heavily upon the Düsseldorf *tableau* presentation, and even in his drawing of the figures he comes close to the exaggerated poses of the characters in Lessing's historical pictures.

Toward the end of the 1840's, the relationship between Düsseldorf and New York grew stronger. The mid-century chronicler of American art, Henry Tuckerman, quoted Leutze in *Artist-Life, Sketches of American Painters*, published in 1847: "For the beginner in the arts Düsseldorf was probably one of the best schools in existence and has educated an uncommon number of distinguished men." Two years later the Düsseldorf Academy received its full-dress recognition in America. Largely through the initiative of John G. Boker, the Prussian Consul in New York, a large group of paintings by members of the Düsseldorf school were brought to America for exhibition. Although the event was prompted by Boker's concern for the safety of the paintings during the uncertain days of the 1848 liberal revolution in Germany, the pictures remained on exhibition from 1849 until 1862 when they were eventually sold at auction.

The opening of the Düsseldorf Gallery in New York was widely and enthusiastically heralded in the press as well as in the publications of the various art associations. The American Art-Union *Bulletin* called it ". . . one of the most gratifying and instructive collections that have ever been seen in the United States. It is full of evidence of that indefatigable and minute study of Form which characterizes the German schools and in regard to which the directors are so exacting, that newly-arrived students are almost reduced to despair by the magnitude of the task before them. But results such as these show the advantage of this severe discipline . . . the decision in handling the freedom of outline, the firmness and accuracy of touch . . . give a completeness and unity to the expression of thought on canvas, which a half-educated artist, however great his genius, can never obtain by his uncertain and tentative experiments."

From the tone of the many reviews concerning the opening of the Düsseldorf Gallery the reader becomes aware that much of the acclaim given the paintings stemmed from the novelty of subject matter and from the abundance of sheer technical ability demonstrated in the various performances by these German artists. Although the School was known for its imposing accomplishments in the field of historical narrative painting—an area untouched by the artists of the native American school—there was also a plentiful sampling of anecdotal genre to be found on the walls of the Düsseldorf Gallery. Hasenclever was represented by a serial treatment of the life of a fictional German university student whose career was traced by events depicted in three episodes. To American eyes such pictures were distinct novelties of subject matter and execution when compared with the most popular of the native school painters such as William S. Mount and John Quidor. The problems inherent in the Düsseldorf approach to genre for a time apparently went undetected by American critics who had been swept up in the general enthusiasm of the moment. Mount's honest observations of life in rural America were technically naive expressions compared to the masterful drawing and painterly finish of an artist like Hasenclever. Yet, the Düsseldorf artists were incapable of the kind of fidelity to life that came naturally to artists like Mount; their's was a form of genre wholly concocted in the studio where sentimental notions about the quality of German peasant life, quite remote from their own middle-class backgrounds, often operated to the exclusion of any chance for a realistic portrayal of their subject matter.

For Richard Caton Woodville, Düsseldorf was an ideal from which he took considerable nourishment for his art. Apparently he neither shared Leutze's aspirations for historical painting nor his misgivings about the dry Düsseldorf style. Although several competent drawings from Woodville's youth attest to his natural talent as a draughtsman, the first solid evidence of his ability comes from the time in the early 1840's when he produced a number of extremely incisive portrait sketches of his teachers and fellow students at the Baltimore alms house. They show Woodville already equipped to engage in a serious pursuit of his art, and his predisposition for genre subjects had already been revealed in a small drawing, *Soldier's Experience*, of 1844 (The Walters Art Gallery). In Düsseldorf he quickly came under the influence of the history painters and by 1847 was turning out paintings in which he struck a balance between elaborate seventeenth-century costume pieces and intimate genre.

Woodville, like Leutze, disengaged from the Academy; after only a year in Düsseldorf, he became the private pupil of Carl Ferdinand Sohn. Sohn had been at the Berlin Academy under Schadow and formerly had painted romantic scenes taken from Renaissance literature to which he imparted a modified Nazarene style. However, his work in Düsseldorf concentrated on portraiture; it was competent without being particularly distinguished. Sohn's most distinguishing quality lay in the clarity of his drawing and color, and, as a teacher, he must be credited with having developed in Woodville a feeling for these qualities.

The Fencing Lesson (Figure 146) indicates a gradual development in Woodville's composition toward the theatrical schema, as much reflected in the costume drama which he presents as it is in the shallow, boxlike setting of the scene. During the following year he produced his two most successful pictures in which he employs compositional devices taken from the Düsseldorf style: *Politics in an Oyster House*, 1848 (The Walters Art Gallery), and *War News from Mexico*, 1848 (National Academy of Design, see Figure 150 for engraving of this work). Both are composed as tightly enclosed units of shallow space, and particularly in *War News* there is given an insistently theatrical treatment, complete with a representation of a miniature stage-like porch upon which the action takes place. Woodville departed from the impassive Düsseldorf manner in the representation of character and animated expression in these two genre pictures, however. As much as *The Fencing Lesson* indicates his attraction to seventeenth-century Dutch rather than German subject matter, so these pictures seem more influenced by the genre style of the Dutch little masters.

It was not until four years later that Woodville revealed himself indebted to the Düsseldorf

Figure III Richard Caton Woodville (American, 1825–1856), *The Sailor's Wedding*, 1852, oil on canvas, h. 18⅛″ × w. 22″ Collection of the Walters Art Gallery, Baltimore, Maryland.

tableau in *The Sailor's Wedding* 1852 (Figure III). Rudolf Jordan, one of the minor teachers at the Academy made a drawing in 1836 (Figure 29) that bears a striking relationship to Woodville's composition and may well have been the inspiration for it. From a stylistic point of view, *The Sailor's Wedding* bears a marked resemblance to the work of Johann Peter Hasenclever. This highly gifted practitioner of the genre idiom had been highly criticized by the administration of the Academy for his intensely realistic portrayals of scenes of contemporary life. Hasenclever avoided the remoteness of the academic ideal and practiced a hearty and often humorous realism in his art; certainly of all the artists associated with the Academy at this time Hasenclever is the one teacher from whom Woodville could have benefited in the production of *The Sailor's Wedding*.

In the spring and summer of 1849, respectively, Worthington Whittredge and Eastman Johnson sailed for Europe; their mutual goal was Düsseldorf and its famous Academy. Whittredge's interest in European art had been kindled by his acquaintance with the collection of Nicholas Longworth in his native Cincinnati. Even before his departure, Whitt-

Figure IV Emanuel Leutze (American, 1816–1868), *Washington Crossing the Delaware*, oil on canvas, h. 149″ × w. 255″ Collection of The Metropolitan Museum of Art, New York, Gift of John S. Kennedy, 1897.

redge had been building a reputation as a landscape painter. He regularly sent paintings to the annual exhibitions of the National Academy of Design, and in 1846 his landscape, *View of the Kanawah, Morning*, was received with acclaim by Asher B. Durand, then president of the Academy. After experiencing the excitement of Paris, Whittredge decided that Düsseldorf, with its quieter, more provincial atmosphere was more suited to his tastes. And as he noted in his *Autobiography*: "I found the professors of the Academy in Düsseldorf among the most liberal-minded artists I ever met, extolling English, French, Belgian, Norwegian and Russian art. The Düsseldorf School, when I reached there, was made up from students of all countries . . . the school, therefore was not alone, the teachings of a few professors in the Academy, but of the whole mass collected . . . and America had Leutze there, the most talked-about artist of them all in 1850."

Leutze's monumental painting, *Washington Crossing the Delaware* (Figure IV), had already acquired a reputation in America some time before its triumphal appearance in New York in September of 1851. Perhaps the partial destruction by fire of the first version, an event duly reported by Leutze himself in a letter published in November 1850 by the Bulletin of *The American Art-Union*, served to heighten the suspense. The painting and the artist's studio had become the focal point for all American artists traveling to Düsseldorf; and reports of the painting's progress were circulated widely by returning travelers. Leutze himself had become something of a political activist during the 1848 struggles for German unity and thus his *Washington* acquired an added symbolic significance, and a timeliness which made possible its acceptance in America "as one of the greatest productions of the age," as Abraham Couzzens, a prominent New York art collector, called it.

26

Whittredge was attracted initially to Düsseldorf's most renowned landscape painter, Andreas Achenbach; but the latter provided him with scant encouragement. Achenbach proved elusive for he did not believe in the efficacy of the studio instruction for the development of young artists. Instead, Whittredge developed a close friendship with Carl Lessing with whom he frequently made sketching trips in the surrounding countryside. Whittredge's style carries a suggestion of the very strong influence of Lessing, particularly noted in the drawings made during the spring of 1852 when the two men made a sketching trip to the Harz mountains. Whittredge was perfectly aware of the shortcomings of the Düsseldorf style whose paintings he described as " . . . colorless and with nothing to recommend them except their design. This was, to be sure, often a compensation for lack of color and the charm of handling it but it was not enough and never will be enough to satisfy us in the realm of art."

But Whittredge was an authentic disciple of the Husdon River School tradition in spite of his exposure to the rhetoric of German painting and the grandeur of Alpine scenery: " . . . it is altogether unsuitable for me, my thoughts ran more upon simple scenes and simple subjects, or it may be I never got into the way of measuring all grandeur in a perpendicular line . . ."

Eastman Johnson made his appearance in Düsseldorf in the fall of 1849 where he immediately enrolled in the Academy and began classes in anatomical drawing. By January of 1851 he had formed a close friendship with Leutze and was " . . . painting under his instruction in an immense atelier . . . with others beside himself, excellent artists and both engaged in large works, forming an atmosphere and an aspect of art not less delightful than it is improving, and I regret now that I had not been with him during my entire stay in Düsseldorf." In another letter Johnson described the object of his activity in Leutze's studio: "Our studio is a large hall where six of us paint with convenience, three on large pictures. The chief is Leutze's of *Washington [Crossing the Delaware]*, 20 feet by 16, figures size of life . . . I am making a copy on a reduced scale from which an engraving is to be made." The Paris art dealers, Goupil, Vibert & Co., who had opened offices in New York under the name of the International Art Union, popularized Leutze's *Washington* by means of this print which sold widely in the United States.

Johnson had worked primarily as a portrait draughtsman, and a comparison between his American work and that accomplished in the first months in Düsseldorf revealed something of the impact this new association had upon him. Where the American drawings were frequently bland in characterization there appears in his German drawings a new sense for dramatic expressiveness. While this shows most vigorously in the portrait of Langhamer (Figure 105) with its quality of romantic introspection, Johnson carried forward this penchant into his work as a genre artist as well. But even though he broke away from Düsseldorf for the Hague in 1851 in order to study, as he said, " . . . the splendid works of Rembrandt and a few other of the old Dutch masters who I find are only to be seen in Holland." Johnson maintained a sobriety in his approach to genre that bears a marked affinity for a Düsseldorf kind of sobriety. Even in the latter part of his career this is to be noted whether it be found in the ambitious conversation piece, *The Hatch Family* of 1871 (The Metropolitan Museum of Art), or in the sunbathed expanses of *The Cranberry Harvest* of 1880 (Timkin Art Gallery).

The Düsseldorf Academy embraced other departments of instruction beyond its traditional center of strength which lay in historical narrative and genre painting. Johnson's companion on the trip to Düsseldorf, George H. Hall, may well have come under the influence of the leading still life painter, Johann W. Preyer, whose work was universally admired for its "extremely graceful fancy." There is in Preyer's sketches (Figures 48, 49) an observation for detail that often imparts a scientific accuracy; yet his finished formal compositions become monumental and somewhat ponderous. The same dichotomy is apparent in the department of landscape in examples of studies of isolated elements of nature such as Oswald Achenbach's *Precipice Near Bozen* (Figure 5) of 1845, a delicate and sensitive drawing by comparison with his heavy paintings of this period. An American landscape painter, James M. Hart, incorporated some of the mannerisms of the Düsseldorf landscape style and continued to explore landscape subjects in this way well into the final quarter of the nineteenth century. His approach carries with it the same dry delineation of form, which like Achenbach's style—and to a certain extent that of the older Johann Schirmer, idealizes nature and does not become involved in minute description. Hart's drawing, *Louella* (Figure 98), is an achievement particularly indebted to the Düsseldorf shorthand notation in point of technique as well as in its conception of composition as a vignette.

Undoubtedly Leutze's fame acted as a magnet, drawing artists to him from as far west in the United States as the Mississippi River. Charles Wimar, born Karl Ferdinand Wimar near Bonn in the Rhineland, had immigrated to America at the age of 15, settling in St. Louis. By 1852 he returned to his native land and became a student of Leutze. While under Leutze's influence, Wimar created a number of paintings and drawings in Düsseldorf which reflected his interest in scenes of wild drama depicting the confrontations of the settlers and the Indians on the western frontier (Figure v). Upon returning to St. Louis in 1856 Wimar became a keen observer of Indian life and shed much of his theatrical Düsseldorf mannerisms. However, one of his final projects, a series of mural decorations for the old courthouse in St. Louis, returned him to a style of painting that is heavily freighted with the grand manner of the Düsseldorf historical style.

In the same year Wimar returned to St. Louis, another artist working in that city went abroad to Düsseldorf. George Caleb Bingham made his pilgrimage as a mature artist rather than as a student, however. His fame as a genre painter had already been well established, having already achieved such masterpieces as *Fur Traders Descending the Missouri*, 1845 (The Metropolitan Museum of Art), *Shooting for the Beef*, 1850 (The Brooklyn Museum), *The Emigration of Daniel Boone*, 1852 (Washington University, St. Louis), and *The Verdict of the People*, 1855 (Boatman's National Bank, St. Louis). Bingham had generous praise for Düsseldorf, writing soon after his arrival: "The striking peculiarity of the school which flourishes here by its own inherent vitality, is a total disregard of the 'old masters' and a direct resort to nature for the truths it employs ... characterized by a freshness, vigor and truth ..." Bingham's intention was not to paint from nature but to create portraits from imagination of Thomas Jefferson and, significantly, of George Washington. Both were destined for the state house in Jefferson City, Missouri. The full-length portrait of Washington, Bingham wrote, was "highly approved by my fellow Americans" and since his studio adjoined that of Leutze it may be assumed that Leutze was among those offering praise. Bingham saw himself as a major competitor with Leutze and had taken the same path toward achieving national

Figure v   Charles Wimar (American, 1828–1862), *The Abduction of Daniel Boone's Daughter by the Indians*, 1853, charcoal and sepia touched with white on paper, h. 36″ × w. 44″. Collection of the St. Louis Art Museum, St. Louis, Missouri.

fame. His *Emigration of Daniel Boone* was also engraved for distribution by Goupil, yet Bingham could not out-distance his rival with this effort. Bingham had begun his own version of *Washington Crossing the Delaware* while still in America, some eight months before his arrival in Düsseldorf. Bingham's version of the scene takes a point of view similar to his Daniel Boone subject with the General and his men shown proceeding directly toward the spectator. The arrangement of figures is characteristic of Bingham's preference for deep space in his paintings; yet his effect in this case is static rather than motive and the picture lacks the majestic frieze-like presentation of Leutze's treatment. The painting remained unfinished until as late as 1872, suggesting Bingham's problems in arriving at an acceptable resolution of this vaunted theme.

A contemporary criticism of the picture singled out "the almost vicious fault" of the coloring: suggesting the adverse effects in that respect of his attempts to produce a picture in the authentic Düsseldorf style. Fortunately, Bingham reverted to his former robust manner of painting in the *Jolly Flat Boatmen in Port* (Figure vi) which he executed in Düsseldorf in 1857 as a re-working of a similar theme of eleven years earlier. Clearly, his feeling for characteriza-

Figure VI   George Caleb Bingham (American, 1811–1879), *The Jolly Flat Boatmen in Port*, 1857, oil on canvas, h. 47½″ × w. 69½″. Collection of the St. Louis Art Museum, St. Louis, Missouri.

tion and his handling of solid form remained untouched by either the sentimental genre of the hard drawing of the Düsseldorf school. The individual figures represented in the painting were assembled from sketches Bingham brought with him from St. Louis (Figs. 87, 88, 89, 90, 91, 92); thus he preserved the authentic flavor of the American scene. Bingham's genre art underwent no changes as a result of his two years in Düsseldorf, for he had not gone there for instruction. Rather, it would seem his appearance in the Rhineland art capital was an obligatory pilgrimage which he undertook in a spirit of deference to the prevailing taste of his time, as much as it seems to have been an unsuccessful attempt to challenge Leutze's supremacy in the field of historical painting.

By the time Bingham returned to St. Louis, the once vaunted strengths of the Düsseldorf school of historical narrative and sentimental genre painting were earning harsh criticism. Where Lessing's *The Martyrdom of Hus* had heaped upon it the most extravagant praise as "one of the grandest productions of modern art before the American public" at the opening of the Düsseldorf Gallery in 1849, this same picture was reduced to being merely "material in the extreme" in the pages of *The Crayon* but nine years later. Similarly, Hasenclever had been acclaimed as a genre painter possessed of a "keen satire and nice discrimination of character" by *The New York Courier* in 1849, but the same pictures were dismissed by *The Crayon*'s critic in 1858 as "pot-house jesting." The judgement that the Düsseldorf school was characterized by the "skeptical mind and materialistic philosophy of nature" came to be the sober evaluation of it: "and this is the end result of material art – to go like those on a treadmill ever laboring, never advancing . . . daily growing more limited, more debased" as *The Crayon* lamented in 1858.

By the time Albert Bierstadt arrived in Düsseldorf sentimental genre painting already had been eclipsed there by a general movement toward greater naturalism in art. Hasenclever died in 1853 and with him ended the strongest element in the genre tradition at Düsseldorf. Landscape painting emerged as the dominant department in the decade of the 1850's. The idealized romantic visions of the older Düsseldorf artists Caspar Scheuren and Johann Schirmer gave way to a greater feeling for objective reality in their treatment of nature. Even in the landscape studies of Carl Lessing there occurs a sharp departure from the idealized forms of his historical subjects. These developments certainly affected the direction of Bierstadt's art, for it had been his intention to study genre painting with Hasenclever.

Bierstadt was born near Düsseldorf, emigrated to America, and in his twenty-third year returned to Germany to pick up family ties, for Hasenclever was his mother's cousin. He naturally gravitated to Leutze's studio with its German-American associations; Charles Wimar had preceded him there by a year, but his closest friend in the Leutze galaxy was Worthington Whittredge, with whom he shared a studio. Whittredge recalled in his *Autobiography*: "After working in my studio for a few months . . . he fitted up a paintbox . . . and shouldering it one cold April morning, he started off to try his luck among the Westphalian peasants . . . He remained away without a word to us until late Autumn when he returned loaded down with innumerable studies of all sorts . . . It was a remarkable summer's work; for anybody who had little or no instruction, it was simply marvelous. He set to work in my studio immediately on large canvases composing and putting together parts of studies he had made . . ."

In one of the sketchbooks Bierstadt kept in 1854 is contained the record of some of this activity; in it is combined a number of drawings of female models posing in native costumes in which the same attitudes are observed as in Woodville's costume study of ten years earlier. However, the difference between the work of these two artists offers ample proof that Bierstadt never was suited temperamentally to the demands of genre painting. By comparison the landscape studies in his sketchbook offer far greater visual interest. Although they be little more than thumbnail sketches, Bierstadt early demonstrated his feeling for dramatic contrasts and effective placement of masses. He seems intuitively to have reached for that peculiarly Düsseldorf habit of composing landscapes as if they existed as a succession of planes parallel with the picture surface. This habit of working continued throughout his career as seen in later pencil sketches, such as *Study of Rocks, Trees by a Lake* (Figure 83), made during his second western trip in 1863, as well as in the drawing entitled *Moselkern* (Figure 84), which he made during his second trip to Europe.

The great sweeping landscapes of the American west, for which Bierstadt later became the most celebrated artist in the field, amply demonstrate his close ties with German romantic painting as much as they tend to repudiate the native American Luminist tradition. Bierstadt diverged from that tradition because he tended to respond to landscape in a visceral way; he discarded the contemplative elements of the Hudson River School style, and raised the panorama idiom to the level of Wagnerian opera. The overtly theatrical effects of Bierstadt's grandiose productions, such as *Rocky Mountains, The Valley of the Yosemite* (engraving reproduced, Figure 85), proclaim his kinship as an artist to the Düsseldorf conception of the idealized landscape. His chief rival, Frederic Church, was the true inheritor of Thomas Cole's introspective approach to nature. Although Bierstadt and Church shared a similar concern for meticulous drawing and the panorama format, they followed divergent paths as landscape painters. Bierstadt satisfied the public's appetite for spectacle, while Church pursued the mysteries of Universal Order in the spirit of what James Jackson Jarves called Nature – "God's sensuous image of revelation."

During the decade of the 1850's many young American artists briefly included Düsseldorf as a point of interest on their tours of Europe. Sanford R. Gifford who was "forcibly struck with the French landscape school" passed through the city in 1855 on his way south to Italy where, in the fall of that year he worked alongside Whittredge and Bierstadt. William Haseltine was attracted to Düsseldorf through the encouragement of his old teacher in Philadelphia, Paul Weber, who had returned to his native land. Haseltine admired the work of Andreas Achenbach with whom he shared an affinity for form especially noted in drawings of the Massachusetts coast like *Nahant–Egg Rock* (Figure 104). But in his early work there exists an occasional parallel effort which demonstrates a close working relationship with his fellow Americans; Haseltine's *Fishing Boats on a Beach* (Figure 103) bears a striking resemblance to similar studies made by Whittredge, for example.

Another Philadelphia artist, William Trost Richards, made a brief appearance in Düsseldorf in 1866. Richards had been to Europe once before in 1853 and had studied in Rome and Paris. Thus, there is a certain mingling of influences in his *Woods* of 1865 (Figure 132) which seems to blend a Barbizon pastoral mood and something of the remains of the Hudson River solemnity. Yet the framing device of the composition with its extremely theatrical aspect also suggests Richards' conscious emulation of Düsseldorf mannerisms. Certainly, his style appears radically changed in the 1867 sketch of Grindelwald (Figure 133) which shows considerably more attention to technical finesse. His work acquired a greater sense of sophistication in the years following; and although he became famous as a painter of seascapes, Richards' most lyrical pictures are to be found in the group of luminous watercolors which he made during the decade of the 1870's (Figures 134, 135, 136).

The era of the Düsseldorf influence in American art came to its quiet close in the decade of the 1860's. Appropriately, it was Emanuel Leutze who provided the *dénouement* to this episode. With the completion of his mural painting, *Westward the Course of Empire Takes its Way* for the U.S. Capitol in 1862, Leutze closed his career as a painter of historical narrative. This ambitious composition received the customary thoroughness of preparation, with a trip to the Rocky Mountains to gather topographic details. This was followed by at least two fully developed scale paintings (Figure VII and Gilcrease Institute, Tulsa). Yet, Leutze's final production on the walls of the Capitol, a scene celebrating the rigors of pioneer emigration and the triumph of territorial conquest, is but a faint echo of his past performances at Düsseldorf. A welter of confusing detail disrupts the composition, and the artist betrays a faltering command of drawing. During the painting of *Westward*, Leutze visited his old friend, Sanford R. Gifford, who was serving in the Union Army and stationed at nearby Camp Cameron. Leutze's sketch of a group of stacked muskets (Figure 123) conveys a feeling of

Figure VII Emanuel Leutze (American, 1816–1868), *Westward the Course of Empire Takes Its Way*, 1861, oil on canvas, h. 33″ × w. 43″. Courtesy of the National Collection of Fine Arts, Smithsonian Institution, Washington, D.C. Bequest of Miss Sara Carr.

realism in contrast with his theatrical mural effort in progress, and at once reveals the essential problems of the studio approach to painting he employed.

Leutze's retreat to the past for subject matter was a predisposition grounded in the Düsseldorf penchant for idealizing history. Thus, Leutze's imagination seems to have been frozen at the moment of great opportunity. The noise of the most tragic and epic battle in American history, Gettysburg, had barely died away when the Pennsylvania Legislature announced a competition open to artists for a mural decoration in the State House at Harrisburg. Leutze apparently did not respond, although he was personally invited by the head of the commission charged with the project. The prize went instead to Frederick P. Rothermel.

Leutze died in 1868, still supported by a reputation earned by his *Washington* of nearly twenty years before. Time dealt harshly with the Düsseldorf artists as well, when their brief moment of exaltation in America had passed.

The influence of the Düsseldorf Academy was marginal when compared to that of the community at large. Certainly our artists were touched by the talents of the prominent instructors of the Academy, and specific instances of Americans having been stimulated thereby have been remarked upon. But, as an international gathering place where artists could exchange ideas and flourish through the interaction of those ideas, Düsseldorf served admirably. More than anything else, however, Düsseldorf was a symbol of professionalism in art; and for American artists who were emerging during the twenty years of its reign over the international scene, Düsseldorf provided them with a sense of belonging to the continuing traditions of the Old World, as much as it offered an escape from provincialism.

Catalogue of the Exhibition

Dimensions are given in inches. Height precedes width.

The German Artists

Unless otherwise noted, all German works are from the Museum of Art, Düsseldorf.

Andreas Achenbach

born, Kassel, in 1815; died, Düsseldorf, in 1910.

Moved with parents to Düsseldorf in 1823. Entered Academy at age 12 and studied with H. C. Kolbe among others. Influenced by Schirmer. Continued independent studies and discovered seventeenth-century Dutch landscapes. Left the Academy in 1835; travelled extensively to Italy, France, Scandinavia, the Netherlands. Was never on the Academy faculty although he settled in Düsseldorf after 1846. The most famous exponent of Düsseldorf landscape painting.

1 *Stormy Seascape*, 1850, pen and bistre ink, $4\frac{3}{8} \times 6$. Lent by Cooper-Hewitt Museum of Decorative Arts and Design, Smithsonian Institution, New York.

2 *Mountainous Landscape*, black crayon, $18\frac{1}{2} \times 12\frac{1}{4}$.

3 *Forest Deep in Snow*, watercolor, tempera, and pencil, $16\frac{5}{8} \times 24\frac{5}{8}$.

Oswald Achenbach

born, Düsseldorf, in 1827; died, Düsseldorf, in 1905.

Influenced by his brother Andreas; studied at the Academy 1839–1841, a pupil of Schirmer. A visit to Italy in 1850 was crucial to his development. Further visits to Italy produced numerous paintings with Italian subjects. Developed a personal style without painstaking quality of Academy. Oswald and his brother, Andreas, were the best known Düsseldorf landscape painters. Taught at the Academy from 1863 to 1872.

4 *Footbridge over a Stream*, 1843, watercolor and pencil, $14\frac{1}{8} \times 19\frac{1}{2}$.

5 *Precipice near Bozen*, 1845, pencil, $9 \times 13\frac{3}{4}$.

6 *Olive Grove near Torbole at Lake Garda*, 1845, pencil, $13\frac{3}{4} \times 19$.

7 *View from Trier (Mosel)*, 1869, watercolor and pencil, $9\frac{1}{2} \times 17\frac{1}{2}$.

8 *Lazzerone (Neapolitan Laborer)*, pencil, $12\frac{3}{4} \times 7\frac{7}{8}$.

Eduard J. F. Bendemann

born, Berlin, in 1811; died, Düsseldorf, in 1889.

Brother-in-law and student of Schadow in Berlin. Followed Schadow to Düsseldorf in 1827 and was one of the master's inner circle. To Rome in 1829–1830. Appointed to Academy in Dresden in 1838. Frescoes for royal family of Saxony in the Palace at Dresden. Appointed Director of Düsseldorf Academy 1859 after Schadow's retirement. Resigned in 1867 but continued teaching activities in his studio. Continued the heroic style of Peter von Cornelius which he sought to combine with characteristics of Schadow's school.

9 *Landscape: Ebermannstadt*, 1854, ink, pencil, and watercolor, $5\frac{5}{8} \times 16\frac{3}{8}$.

10 *Portrait of Ludwig Richter*, 1858, black crayon, $20\frac{1}{4} \times 15\frac{1}{8}$.

11 *Wilhelm von Schadow on his Sickbed*, 1860, black and yellow crayon, $22 \times 17\frac{3}{4}$.

12 *Portrait of a Man*, 1860, black and white crayon, $17\frac{1}{2} \times 14\frac{3}{8}$.

13 *Study for a Wall Painting*, grey ink and black crayon, $10\frac{3}{4} \times 8\frac{5}{8}$.

14 *Grape Harvest—Study for a Wall Painting*, gray ink and black crayon, $10\frac{3}{4} \times 8\frac{5}{8}$.

Christian Eduard Boettcher

born, Ingenbroich, in 1818; died, Düsseldorf, in 1889.

Student at the Academy 1844–1849 under Hildebrandt and Schadow. Favorite subjects were amiable presentations of rural idyl. Active lithographer.

15 *Children Returning from Gathering Leaves*, 1850, pencil and watercolour, $8\frac{1}{4} \times 10\frac{3}{4}$.

16 *Lovers at the Wall*, 1853, pencil, 10×8.

Wilhelm Camphausen

born, Düsseldorf, in 1818; died, Düsseldorf, in 1885.

Studied at the Academy from 1834 under Sohn and Schadow, Rethel, and Lessing. Painted scenes from German history of seventeenth, eighteenth and nineteenth centuries. Accurate observer of detail and characteristics of subject.

17 *Picnic near Ratingen*, 1857, pencil, $3\frac{1}{4} \times 5\frac{7}{8}$.

18 *Landscape near a Lake*, 1866, pencil and tempera, $9 \times 11\frac{1}{2}$.

19 *A Rest in the Grafenberg Forest*, 1867, pencil, $3\frac{1}{2} \times 6$.

20 *The Hunt—Tristan Sings his Life Story*, pencil, $15\frac{3}{8} \times 24\frac{7}{8}$.

Ernst Deger

born, near Hildesheim, in 1809; died, Düsseldorf, in 1885.

Studied at Berlin Academy in 1828; enrolled in Düsseldorf Academy in 1829 and worked under guidance of Schadow. Part of a group under influence of Nazarenes in their religious history paintings. In Italy 1837–1841; participated in the Nazarene project of wall decorations in Apollinaris Church in Remagen. Much admired in Düsseldorf and beyond. Member of Berlin Academy in 1849. Appointed professor of religious history painting at Düsseldorf Academy in 1869.

21 *Study for a Crucifixion*, pencil, heightened with white, $13\frac{7}{8} \times 11\frac{3}{8}$.

22 *Figure and Hand Studies*, pencil, heightened with white, $16\frac{1}{8} \times 12$.

Jacob F. Dielmann

born, near Frankfurt, in 1809; died, Frankfurt, in 1885.

Studied in Frankfurt 1825–1827; on a grant to Düsseldorf Academy in 1835. Studied landscape painting under Schirmer. Returned to Frankfurt in 1842 taking with him the best aspects of Düsseldorf painting. Specialized in landscape and rural genre, and was active as an illustrator. Dielmann was an independent colorist which led him into directions parallel to contemporary French landscape artists.

23 *Study of a Woman*, pencil and wash, $11\frac{3}{8} \times 8\frac{5}{8}$.

Johann Peter Hasenclever

born, Remscheid, in 1810; died, Düsseldorf, in 1853.

Student at the Academy after 1827, first as architect, then as painter. At first rejected by Schadow but after independent studies again was accepted at the Academy. After travels to Munich and Italy, settled in Düsseldorf in 1842 where he became much admired.

24 *Munich Beerhall*, 1842, pencil and brown ink, $14\frac{7}{8} \times 18\frac{1}{2}$.

25 *The Winetasters*, pencil and brown ink, $11\frac{1}{8} \times 14\frac{1}{2}$.

26 *An Artist's Studio* (central figure is Hasenclever), black crayon, with traces of white, $24 \times 35\frac{1}{2}$.

27 *A Travelling Company*, ink and pencil, $10\frac{5}{8} \times 14\frac{1}{2}$.

Ferdinand Theodor Hildebrandt

born, Stettin, in 1804; died, Düsseldorf, in 1874.

Became student of Berlin Academy in 1820; pupil of Schadow in 1823 whom he accompanied to Düsseldorf in 1826. Was a member of Schadow's inner circle. Traveled to Belgium, Italy, and Russia. Assistant teacher at the Academy in 1832, appointed professor and successor to H. C. Kolbe in 1836. Resigned in 1854 because of emotional disturbances. A leading exponent of romantic-poetic direction of the Academy. Hildebrandt's superior technique and his personal style made him one of the most influential artists at the Academy.

28 *Portrait of a Lady*, 1864, pencil, $8\frac{1}{2} \times 6\frac{5}{8}$.

Rudolf Jordan

born, Berlin, in 1810; died, Düsseldorf, in 1887.

At first self-taught; enrolled at Academy in 1833; studied with Schadow and Sohn until 1840.
Member of the Master Class until 1848. Traveled to North Germany, Holland, Belgium, and Normandy; became painter of fisherfolk whom he painted with sympathy and humor and usually without Düsseldorf sentimentality. Published lithographs and etchings.

29 *The Wedding Procession*, 1836, pencil and ink, $9\frac{1}{2} \times 11\frac{1}{2}$.

30 *Women Awaiting the Return of the Fishermen*, 1852, pencil, $11\frac{7}{8} \times 18\frac{1}{2}$.

Carl Friedrich Lessing

born, Breslau, in 1808; died, Karlsruhe, in 1880.

Began his studies in Berlin in 1822; moved to Düsseldorf in 1826 as a pupil of Schadow. While not a member of the Academy faculty, he was among influential artists in Düsseldorf in the field of history painting and landscape. Appointed professor at the Art School of Karlsruhe in 1858.

31 *Mountain Landscape in a Storm*, 1825, pen, ink, sepia wash, opaque white, $14\frac{9}{16} \times 12\frac{9}{16}$
Lent by the Cincinnati Art Museum.

32 *Study for "The Storming of Iconium,"* 1831, ink, pencil and watercolor, $14\frac{3}{4} \times 18\frac{3}{4}$.

33 *Walther and Hildegunde*, 1834, ink and pencil, $17\frac{1}{2} \times 20\frac{1}{2}$

34 *Crusader's Watch*, 1834–1835, ink, pencil, watercolor, and crayon, $19\frac{1}{8} \times 24\frac{7}{8}$.

35 *Jan Hus before the Council of Constance*, 1845, sepia wash, $18\frac{1}{4} \times 26\frac{3}{4}$
Lent by the Museum of Fine Arts, Boston, Gift of the Estate of Mrs. James H. Beal.

36 *Family Portrait*, 1845, pencil, $13\frac{1}{2} \times 17\frac{1}{4}$.

37 *The Crusaders Find a Spring in the Desert*, 1849, pencil, pen and ink, gray wash, $20\frac{1}{4} \times 26\frac{3}{8}$
Lent by the Cincinnati Art Museum.

38 *Rocky Landscape in the Harz Mountains: Regenstein*, 1852, pencil, watercolor and opaque white, 11×19.
Lent by the Cincinnati Art Museum.

39 *Hills and Fields: Michelstein*, 1852, pencil, charcoal and watercolor, $10\frac{7}{8} \times 16\frac{15}{16}$
Lent by the Cincinnati Art Museum.

40 *Near Halberstadt*, 1852, pencil, watercolor, charcoal and opaque white, $10\frac{3}{8} \times 16\frac{7}{8}$
Lent by the Cincinnati Art Museum.

41 *Rocky Hill and Forest: Michelstein*, 1852, charcoal and watercolor, $11\frac{7}{8} \times 18\frac{3}{16}$
Lent by the Cincinnati Art Museum.

42 *Portrait of Worthington Whittredge*, 1853, pencil, charcoal, wash and white chalk, $14\frac{5}{8} \times 11\frac{7}{8}$
Lent by the Cincinnati Art Museum.

43 *Tree Study*, 1853, pencil, charcoal, gray-brown wash, opaque yellow, $23\frac{5}{8} \times 18\frac{11}{16}$
Lent by the Cincinnati Art Museum.

44 *Old Man in a Monk's Robe*, pencil, charcoal, wash, red crayon, $21\frac{9}{16} \times 17\frac{5}{16}$
Lent by the Cincinnati Art Museum.

45 *The Capture of Pope Paschal II*, pencil, $3\frac{1}{8} \times 5\frac{1}{8}$.

Heinrich Carl Anton Mücke

born, Breslau, in 1806; died, Düsseldorf, in 1891.

Studied in Breslau and after 1824 under Schadow whom he accompanied to Düsseldorf in 1826. Traveled to Rome and England. Taught at Academy 1844–1867. Mücke, Hildebrandt, and Lessing were the most important history painters in Düsseldorf.

46 *St. Hubert*, 1836, pencil and brown ink, heightened with white, $7\frac{1}{2} \times 6\frac{7}{8}$.

47 *Hunter and Nymph*, dark brown ink, $7\frac{1}{4} \times 8\frac{1}{4}$.

Johann Wilhelm Preyer

born, Rheydt, in 1803; died, Düsseldorf, in 1889.

Both he and his brother, the landscape painter Gustav Preyer, were dwarfs. Enrolled in Düsseldorf Academy in 1822, first as student of Peter von Cornelius, later under Wilhelm von Schadow. From 1828 active as a landscape and still life painter. Visited Holland in 1835, later Munich, and Italy; traveled with Hasenclever. Extensive studies of different fruits; small paintings under seventeenth-century Dutch influence rendered with great precision and considered among the best draughtsmen in Düsseldorf.

48 *Studies of Plants*, 1833, pencil, $7\frac{1}{2} \times 10\frac{3}{4}$.

49 *Still Life*, 1880, ink and watercolor, $10\frac{5}{8} \times 13\frac{3}{4}$.

Alfred Rethel

born, near Aachen, in 1816; died, Düsseldorf, in 1859.

His superior draughtsmanship evident in his early years. Enrolled in the Academy at age 13, studied there until 1836 under Kolbe, Hildebrandt, and Schadow; and influenced by Lessing. Continued studies in Frankfurt where he shed the Nazarene influence in his work as history painter. Traveled to Italy; active in Aachen, Düsseldorf, and Dresden. Emotionally disturbed after 1853.

50 *Study for a Monk with a Cross*, charcoal and pastel, $18\frac{3}{8} \times 11\frac{7}{8}$.

51 *The Baptism of Widukind*, pencil and wash, $5\frac{5}{8} \times 3\frac{5}{8}$.

52 *The Destruction of Jerusalem*, pencil and ink, $6\frac{3}{8} \times 3\frac{7}{8}$.

Henry Ritter

born, Montreal, in 1816; died, Düsseldorf, in 1853.

Son of British army officer. Came to Düsseldorf in 1836 as student of Sohn. Worked with Rudolf Jordan.

53 *The Artist's Children*, 1846, pencil and watercolor, $14\frac{1}{2} \times 15\frac{3}{4}$.

54 *The Last of the Mohicans*, pencil, $10\frac{7}{8} \times 8\frac{3}{8}$.

55 *In the Studio*, pencil, $8\frac{1}{4} \times 7\frac{1}{8}$.

Friedrich Wilhelm von Schadow

born, Berlin, in 1788; died, Düsseldorf, in 1862.

Son of J. G. Schadow, sculptor and director of Berlin Academy who gave him early training. Enrolled in Berlin Academy in 1808. To Rome in 1810; became a Catholic; worked with Cornelius, Overbeck, and other Nazarenes on frescoes in the Casa Bartholdy. Returned to Berlin in 1819 and appointed Academy Professor. Succeeded Cornelius as Director of Düsseldorf Academy in 1826 and made the School one of the leading centers of the time. Received many honors and was knighted in 1845. Retired in 1859 for health reasons.

56 *Study for a Portrait of Banker Fraenkel's Daughter*, 1824–1825, black and white crayon and brush, $12\frac{3}{8} \times 10$.

57 *Floating Figure of a Woman*, black, red, white and yellow crayon, $25 \times 19\frac{1}{2}$.

58 *Floating Figure of a Woman*, black, red and white crayon, $24\frac{3}{4} \times 19\frac{1}{4}$.

Caspar J. N. Scheuren

born, Aachen, in 1810; died, Düsseldorf, in 1887.

Trained as a painter by his father; studied at Academy from 1829 under influence of Schirmer and Lessing; appointed professor in 1855; received commissions from the Prussian royal family. Executed painterly, romantic landscapes from the Rhine valley.

59 *The Four Seasons: Spring*, 1865, watercolor, $12 \times 18\frac{1}{2}$
Lent by the Cincinnati Art Museum.

60 *The Four Seasons: Summer*, 1865, watercolor, $12 \times 18\frac{1}{2}$
Lent by the Cincinnati Art Museum.

61 *The Four Seasons: Autumn*, 1865, watercolor, $12 \times 18\frac{1}{2}$
Lent by the Cincinnati Art Museum.

62 *The Four Seasons: Winter*, 1865, watercolor, $12 \times 18\frac{1}{2}$
Lent by the Cincinnati Art Museum.

63 *Ruins on the Rhine*, pencil and brown wash, $23\frac{1}{4} \times 18\frac{7}{8}$.

Johann Wilhelm Schirmer

born, Jülich, in 1807; died, Karlsruhe, in 1863.

Self-taught until he enrolled in Academy in 1825 as pupil of Cornelius and Kolbe. Early interest in landscape. Traveled with Lessing; visited Italy in 1839–1840. Influence of the work of Poussin and Lorrain became crucial to his development; close study of German landscape. Teacher at Academy in 1833 and appointed professor in 1839; established new department of landscape at the Academy and became one of the most influential artists there. Appointed director of the Art School at Karlsruhe in 1854.

64 *View into the Park of the Villa Borghese*, 1839–1840, pencil and tempera, $16\frac{7}{8} \times 22$.

65 *Cypresses*, 1840, watercolor, $22\frac{3}{4} \times 17\frac{3}{8}$.

66 *Hessian Landscape*, 1849, ink over traces of pencil and tempera, $22\frac{1}{4} \times 27\frac{1}{2}$.

67 *Landscape with the Flight into Egypt*, ink, pencil and watercolor, $12\frac{1}{4} \times 16\frac{1}{4}$.

68 *Forest Landscape with an Aqueduct*, charcoal, $17\frac{3}{8} \times 24\frac{3}{4}$.

69 *Landscape*, brown and white crayon, $15\frac{1}{2} \times 21$.

Adolf Schroedter

born, Schwedt, in 1805; died, Karlsruhe, in 1875.

Trained by his father as an etcher; continued studies at Berlin Academy after 1820. Came to Düsseldorf in 1829 to study with Schadow. Lived briefly in London, then Frankfurt; returned to Düsseldorf in 1854. Professor in draughtsmanship in Karlsruhe in 1859. Schroedter was known for his humorous depictions of rural folk, also comical figures from literature. He was an active illustrator and printmaker. Influenced Adolph von Menzel, J. C. Sonderland.

70 *The Winetasting*, 1850, watercolor and pencil, $7\frac{7}{8} \times 5\frac{7}{8}$.

Arnold Schulten

born, Düsseldorf, in 1809; died, Düsseldorf, in 1874.

Student at the Academy in landscape painting under Schirmer.

71 *Romantic Landscape with a Castle*, 1835, ink, watercolor and pencil, $11\frac{1}{8} \times 9$.

72 *Landscape with Worshippers*, 1868, watercolor and pencil, $5\frac{1}{8} \times 8$.

Carl Ferdinand Sohn

born, Berlin, in 1805; died, Cologne, in 1867.

Student of Schadow's in Berlin in 1823. Accompanied Schadow to Düsseldorf in 1826. Visited Italy 1830–1831 with Schadow and other Düsseldorf artists. Trip was of great importance to his development. Admired portrait painter and represented the poetic-romantic direction in Düsseldorf. Taught at Academy 1832–1852; influential among Düsseldorf artists.

73 *Two Young Ladies*, 1850, pencil, $7\frac{1}{4} \times 8\frac{1}{4}$.

Johann Baptist Sonderland

born, Düsseldorf, in 1805; died, Düsseldorf, in 1878.

Student at Academy under Cornelius and Schadow. Active as genre painter, illustrator and printmaker.

74 *The Sermon of Jan Hus*, (drawing after Lessing's painting), 1835, pencil and wash, $9\frac{3}{8} \times 11\frac{3}{4}$.

75 *The Farewell*, watercolor, tempera and pencil, $13\frac{1}{4} \times 11$.

Wilhelm Volkhardt

born, Herdicke, in 1815; died, Düsseldorf, in 1876.

Student at Düsseldorf Academy 1831–1840. Traveled to Italy in 1846. Settled in Düsseldorf as painter of themes from the Bible and history.

76 *Head and Hand Studies*, pencil, $10 \times 12\frac{1}{4}$.

J. B. W. August Weber

born, Frankfurt, in 1817; died, Düsseldorf, in 1873.

Studied in Frankfurt and Darmstadt; in Düsseldorf under Schirmer, 1838–1839. Produced idealized landscapes with sensitive treatment of light and mood. Member of the Berlin Academy. Taught in his own studio in Düsseldorf.

77 *Study of a Tree*, wash and pencil, $13\frac{3}{8} \times 10$.

78 *Landscape*, pencil and crayon, $18\frac{3}{4} \times 12\frac{3}{4}$.

The American Artists

Albert Bierstadt

born, Solingen, Germany, in 1830; died, New York City, in 1902.

Brought by his parents to New Bedford, Massachusetts in 1831–1832, Bierstadt returned to Germany in 1853 to study at the Düsseldorf Academy with Lessing, Leutze, and Andreas Achenbach. Remained in Europe until 1857, traveling in Germany, Switzerland and Italy. Back in the United States, he served as an artist with General F. W. Lander's survey expedition to the west, 1859 (the first of four western trips). Settled in New York in 1860; elected to the National Academy the same year. From 1866 to 1882, lived in Irvington-on-the-Hudson, then, aside from several more visits to Europe, settled in New York.

79 *Sketchbook* (fifteen double pages), 1853, pencil, heightened with white, book: $8 \times 5\frac{3}{8}$, page: $7\frac{13}{16} \times 4\frac{3}{8}$
Lent by The Addison Gallery of American Art, Phillips Academy, Andover, Massachusetts.

80 *Study made in Germany* (two views of a bearded peasant, seated), ca. 1853, pencil and chalk, $8\frac{1}{8} \times 12\frac{3}{4}$
Collection of Mr. and Mrs. Maurice Glickman.

81 *German Costume Study* (seated peasant woman), ca. 1853, crayon, wash, and chalk, $13\frac{3}{8} \times 9\frac{1}{2}$
Collection of Mr. and Mrs. Maurice Glickman.

82 *Study of a Ewe*, ca. 1855, pencil, crayon, and chalk, $10\frac{1}{4} \times 13$
Collection of Mr. and Mrs. Maurice Glickman.

83 *Study of Rocks and Trees by a Lake*, ca. 1863, pencil, 11×15
Lent by Florence Lewison Gallery, New York.

84 *Moselkern, Germany*, 1864 (1867–1868?), pencil and chalk, $10 \times 16\frac{3}{4}$
Lent by Florence Lewison Gallery, New York.

85 *Rocky Mountain, The Valley of the Yosemite*, 1866, engraving after Albert Bierstadt by James Smillie
Lent by The Library of Congress, Washington.

George Caleb Bingham

born, Augusta County, Virginia, in 1811; died, Kansas City, in 1879.

When Bingham was eight, his family moved to Missouri, where he lived most of his life. Studied art at the Pennsylvania Academy in 1837. Spent four years in Washington, D.C., 1840–1844. Was a student at Düsseldorf from 1856 to 1858, and again in 1859. Back in Missouri after his last sojourn in Europe, became a well-known politician, portraitist, and genre painter primarily of political scenes. Appointed professor of art at the University of Missouri in 1877.

86 *Seated Man in a Broad-brimmed Hat*, 1836, pencil and wash, $7\frac{7}{16} \times 9\frac{5}{16}$
Lent by the Museum of Fine Arts, Boston, M. and M. Karolik Collection.

87 *Man Standing with Pipe*, ca. 1857, pencil and other media, $10\frac{5}{8} \times 6\frac{1}{2}$
Lent by the St. Louis Mercantile Library Association, John How Collection.

88 *Pan Player*, pencil and other media, $13\frac{5}{8} \times 8\frac{7}{8}$
Lent by the St. Louis Mercantile Library Association, John How Collection.

89 *Fiddler*, pencil and other media, $15\frac{1}{4} \times 11\frac{1}{4}$
Lent by the St. Louis Mercantile Library Association, John How Collection.

90 *Man with Pipe, Seated*, pencil and other media, $9\frac{1}{2} \times 8\frac{1}{2}$
Lent by the St. Louis Mercantile Library Association, John How Collection.

91 *Spectator Seated, Back View*, pencil, $10\frac{7}{8} \times 8\frac{3}{8}$
Lent by the St. Louis Mercantile Library Association, John How Collection.

92 *Spectator Seated, Front View*, pencil and other media, $9\frac{3}{4} \times 8\frac{1}{4}$
Lent by the St. Louis Mercantile Library Association, John How Collection.

James McDougal Hart

born, Kilmarnock, Scotland, in 1828; died, Brooklyn, New York, in 1901.

Brought by his family to the United States when he was three years old. His older brother was the painter William Hart. Lived in Albany, New York, where his apprenticeship to a sign painter aroused an interest in art. Went to Munich and then to Düsseldorf to study painting under Schirmer from 1850 to 1853. Living in New York from 1857, Hart became a frequent exhibitor at major eastern galleries. Elected a member of the National Academy, 1860; later became its vice-president. Married an amateur painter, Marie Theresa Gorsuch, in 1866. William Gorsuch Hart, their son, also became an artist.

93 *Still Life*, 1856, pencil, $7\frac{1}{4} \times 11\frac{1}{4}$
Lent by Dr. William H. Gerdts, New York.

94 *Trees and Stream*, 1861, pencil, heightened with white, $15\frac{3}{4} \times 12\frac{3}{4}$
Lent by Mr. and Mrs. Gudmund Vigtel.

95 *Tree and Picket Fence*, 1863, pencil, $13 \times 16\frac{3}{4}$
Lent by The High Museum of Art, Atlanta, Museum purchase with funds from the Members Guild, 1971.

96 *Cows Resting*, 1871, pencil and chalk, $10\frac{1}{2} \times 13\frac{3}{4}$
Lent by Florence Lewison Gallery, New York.

97 *Study of Sheep*, 1872, pencil and chalk, 12×18
Collection of Mr. and Mrs. Maurice Glickman.

98 *Louella*, 1879, pencil, $19\frac{5}{8} \times 12\frac{9}{16}$
Lent by the Museum of Fine Arts, Boston, M. and M. Karolik Collection.

William Stanley Haseltine

born, Philadelphia, in 1835; died, Rome, in 1900.

Studied in Philadelphia under Paul Weber for two years, then went to Harvard. After graduating from Harvard in 1854, traveled to Düsseldorf to study with Andreas Achenbach at the Academy. In 1856, accompanied by Emanuel Leutze, Worthington Whittredge, and Albert Bierstadt on a sketching trip up the Rhine and also to Italy. Settled in New York in 1858; elected to the National Academy in 1859. To Paris in 1866, then Rome, where, except for a four-year stay in the United States (1895–1899), he settled permanently.

99 *Oleavana—Campagna Romana*, 1858, ink and wash, $14\frac{7}{16} \times 20\frac{1}{2}$
Lent by The Metropolitan Museum of Art, Purchase, Rogers Fund, 1967.

100 *Tivoli*, 1858, ink and wash, $17\frac{1}{4} \times 22\frac{7}{8}$
Lent by The Metropolitan Museum of Art, Gift of Mrs. Rogers Plowden, 1967.

101 *Blankenbergh*, 1876, gouache, $20\frac{7}{8} \times 14\frac{1}{4}$
Lent by the Corcoran Gallery of Art, Washington.

102 *Olive Grove at Tivoli*, pencil, heightened with white, $14\frac{3}{4} \times 21\frac{1}{8}$
Lent by the William Hayes Fogg Art Museum, Harvard University, Cambridge, Massachusetts, Gift of Helen Haseltine Plowden.

103 *Fishing Boats on a Beach*, pencil and watercolor, $14\frac{1}{2} \times 21$
Lent by the William Hayes Fogg Art Museum, Harvard University, Cambridge, Massachusetts, Gift of Helen Haseltine Plowden.

104 *Nahant—Egg Rock*, pencil and watercolor, $13\frac{5}{8} \times 21\frac{7}{8}$
Lent by The High Museum of Art, Atlanta, Gift of Helen Haseltine Plowden, daughter of the artist, 1952.

Eastman Johnson

born, Lovell, Maine, in 1824; died, New York, in 1906.

In 1840, worked for about a year in a Boston lithography shop; then took up crayon portraiture, working in that medium in Boston, in 1840–1844, Washington, D.C. 1844–1845, and Cambridge, Mass. in 1846–1849. To Düsseldorf in 1849, where he studied anatomical drawing at the Academy. Remained in Düsseldorf, entering Leutze's studio in 1851. Went to London and and the Hague in the summer of 1851 where he stayed until 1855. studied briefly with Thomas Couture in Paris in 1855 and returned to the United States that year to work in Washington, D.C., and Superior, Wisconsin until 1857. Worked in Cincinnati, 1857–1858, and settled permanently in New York in 1858. Elected to National Academy in 1860. During first years of the Civil War, followed Union Army on several campaigns. Spent many summers after 1870 painting landscape and genre scenes on Nantucket. Painted mostly portraits in his later years.

105 *Portrait of Langhamer*, 1849, charcoal, $23\frac{5}{8} \times 18\frac{3}{4}$
Lent by the Museum of Fine Arts, Boston, M. and M. Karolik Collection.

106 *Colonel Lottner*, 1850, pencil and sepia wash, 9×8
Lent by Kennedy Galleries, New York.

107 *Three Dutch Figures*, ca. 1852, watercolor and pencil, $6\frac{1}{2} \times 10\frac{7}{8}$
Collection of Mr. and Mrs. Maurice Glickman.

108 *Counterfeiters*, 1854, charcoal, $12 \times 15\frac{3}{4}$
Lent by Mr. and Mrs. Ralph Spencer, New York.

109 *Study of an Oriental*, ca. 1851–1855, pencil, $21\frac{1}{4} \times 15$
Lent by the Museum of Fine Arts, Boston,
M. and M. Karolik Collection.

110 *Polly Gary*, 1855, charcoal and chalk, $18\frac{1}{2} \times 14$
Lent by The Addison Gallery of American Art,
Phillips Academy, Andover, Massachusetts.

111 *Secretary Dobbins*, 1856, charcoal, 27×19
Lent by The Addison Gallery of American Art,
Phillips Academy, Andover, Massachusetts.

112 *Old Woman and Child*, ca. 1860, ink, charcoal and
white chalk, 21×16
Lent by Hirschl and Adler Galleries, Inc.,
New York.

113 *Husking*, 1875, pencil and watercolor, $18\frac{3}{4} \times 12\frac{1}{4}$
Lent by the Free Library of Philadelphia.

114 *Captain Myrick*, 1880, charcoal, $10\frac{3}{4} \times 6\frac{3}{4}$
Lent by the Free Library of Philadelphia.

115 *Richard Peters*, charcoal, $15\frac{3}{4} \times 11\frac{7}{8}$
Lent by the Corcoran Gallery of Art, Washington.

116 *Berry Picking*, 1875–1880, watercolor, $7\frac{3}{4} \times 19\frac{3}{8}$
Lent by The Addison Gallery of American Art,
Phillips Academy, Andover, Massachusetts.

Emanuel Gottlieb Leutze

born, Gmünd, in 1816; died,
Washington, D.C., in 1868.

Brought to America as a child and raised in
Philadelphia. In 1841, to the Düsseldorf Academy
to study with Carl Friedrich Lessing. Traveled to
Munich (1842), Venice, and Rome. Became a
prominent teacher at Düsseldorf, where he settled
from 1845 to 1859. Was a founder of the "Malkasten" in 1848. Painted one of the most famous
pictures to come from the Academy, *Washington
Crossing the Delaware*, 1850. Returned to the United
States in 1859 to paint a mural, *Westward the
Course of Empire Takes Its Way*, for the House of
Representatives. Spent the last ten years of his life
in Washington and New York.

117 *Cathedral Ruins*, ca. 1845, watercolor, $10\frac{1}{2} \times 14\frac{1}{2}$
Lent by the Corcoran Gallery of Art, Washington.

118 *Study of Eastman Johnson*, 1850, brown crayon,
$20 \times 16\frac{3}{4}$
Lent by the Museum of Fine Arts, Boston, M. and
M. Karolik Collection.

119 *Preaching to the Indians*, 1852, pencil, $12\frac{3}{16} \times 8\frac{5}{16}$
Lent by the Corcoran Gallery of Art, Washington.

120 *David Playing before Saul*, 1853, pencil, $7\frac{3}{4} \times 5\frac{5}{8}$
Lent by the Corcoran Gallery of Art, Washington.

121 *The Soldier's Farewell*, 1859, pen and sepia ink,
$9\frac{3}{4} \times 7\frac{11}{16}$
Lent by The Metropolitan Museum of Art,
Gift of James C. McGuire, 1926.

122 *Study for "Westward the Course of Empire Takes Its
Way,"* ca. 1860, pencil, $12\frac{1}{4} \times 19$
Lent by the Corcoran Gallery of Art, Washington.

123 *Seventh Regiment, Camp Cameron, Stacked Rifles*,
1861, pencil, $8\frac{3}{4} \times 5\frac{3}{8}$
Lent by The Library of Congress, Washington.

124 *Gold Mining, Central City*, 1861, watercolor, $14 \times 10\frac{3}{8}$
Lent by the Museum of Fine Arts, Boston, M. and
M. Karolik Collection.

125 *Studies with Washington's Head*, pen with wash,
$9 \times 7\frac{11}{16}$
Lent by the Museum of Fine Arts, Boston, M. and
M. Karolik Collection.

126 *Leutze, Painting (Self-Caricature)*, pencil, $8\frac{3}{8} \times 5$
Lent by The Library of Congress, Washington.

127 *The Dear Lumpish Baby*, pencil, $8\frac{3}{8} \times 10$
Lent by The Library of Congress, Washington.

128 *Landscape in Thundershower*, gray wash, $8\frac{3}{8} \times 5$
Lent by The Library of Congress, Washington.

129 *Hind Quarters of a Horse*, watercolor, $7\frac{1}{4} \times 4\frac{5}{8}$
Lent by The Library of Congress, Washington.

130 *Head of a Girl in a Hat*, pencil, $7\frac{1}{4} \times 4\frac{5}{8}$
Lent by The Library of Congress, Washington.

131 *The Last Drop*, pencil and ink, $5\frac{1}{4} \times 4\frac{3}{4}$
Lent by The Metropolitan Museum of Art,
Gift of James C. McGuire, 1926.

William Trost Richards

born, Philadelphia, in 1833; died, Newport,
Rhode Island, in 1905.

Richards was first a designer of gas fixtures and
chandeliers. Studied with Paul Weber in Philadelphia in 1853, and in the same year went abroad
to study painting in Florence, Rome, and Paris.
Influenced by Ruskin's art theories. In 1856, returned to settle in Germantown, Pennsylvania. To
Düsseldorf and Darmstadt in 1866 for further
study. About 1867, turned predominantly to the
painting of coast scenes and seascapes. Made
frequent trips to the British Isles, and elsewhere.
Settled permanently in Newport in 1890.

132 *Woods*, 1865, charcoal heightened with white,
24×29
Lent by The High Museum of Art, Atlanta,
Museum purchase with funds from The Charles E.
Merrill Trust given in memory of Brigadier
General William L. Plummer, 1972.

133 *Grindelwald, Switzerland*, 1867, pencil, $9\frac{1}{8} \times 11\frac{5}{8}$
Lent by the Museum of Fine Arts, Boston, M. and
M. Karolik Collection.

134 *Franconia Mountains from Compton, New Hampshire*,
1872, watercolor, $8\frac{3}{16} \times 14\frac{3}{16}$
Lent by The Metropolitan Museum of Art, Gift of
Rev. E. L. Magoon, 1880.

135 *Baldart Castle*, 1892, watercolor, 15 × 25
Lent by the Corcoran Gallery of Art, Washington,
Bequest of George E. Lemon.

136 *East Hampton Beach*, watercolor, 18 × 32
Lent by The High Museum of Art, Atlanta, Gift of
Mr. and Mrs. Emory Cocke, 1970.

Worthington Whittredge

born, Springfield, Ohio, in 1820; died, Summit,
New Jersey, in 1910.

Largely self-taught as a portrait painter in Cincinnati, and Indianapolis, until, in 1849, went to
study in Düsseldorf. While there, posed for several
figures in Leutze's painting, *Washington Crossing
the Delaware*; and was closely associated with
Andreas Achenbach, in whose home he stayed for
a year. Left Düsseldorf in 1854 and made sketching
trip through Switzerland and Italy. Lived in
Rome from 1855 until his return to New York in
1859. In 1866, he accompanied the Pope Expedition
to Colorado and New Mexico. Four years later he
went west again, this time in the company of
Sanford Gifford and John Kensett. Moved to
Summit, New Jersey, in 1880. Elected to the
National Academy in 1861; president of the Academy, 1865, and 1874–1877.

137 *Sketch from Nature*, 1853, pencil with brown wash,
$13\frac{1}{2} \times 19\frac{3}{4}$
Lent by The Addison Gallery of American Art,
Phillips Academy, Andover, Massachusetts.

138 *Study of Three Boats*, 1856, watercolor, $11\frac{11}{16} \times 16\frac{15}{16}$
Lent by the Museum of Fine Arts, Boston,
M. and M. Karolik Collection.

139 *Isola dei Pescatori, Lago Maggiore*, 1857, pencil,
$12\frac{3}{4} \times 18\frac{7}{8}$
Lent by the Museum of Fine Arts, Boston, M. and
M. Karolik Collection.

140 *View of Lake and Houses*, ca. 1857, pencil, $12\frac{3}{4} \times 19$
Lent by the Corcoran Gallery of Art, Washington.

141 *Study of a Tree*, 1871, pencil, $15 \times 11\frac{5}{8}$
Lent by the Museum of Fine Arts, Boston, M. and
M. Karolik Collection.

142 *Bishop Berkeley's House, Newport, Rhode Island*,
1877, pencil, $15\frac{1}{4} \times 22\frac{3}{16}$
Lent by the Museum of Fine Arts, Boston, M. and
M. Karolik Collection.

143 *Hillside, Group of Figures Outside a Row of Houses*,
pencil, $12\frac{3}{4} \times 19$
Lent by the Corcoran Gallery of Art, Washington.

144 *Sketch from "Crossing the Ford, Platte River, Colorado,"*
watercolor, $9\frac{1}{2} \times 13\frac{1}{2}$
Lent by Mrs. Catherine Maynard, Atlanta.

Richard Caton Woodville

born, Baltimore, in 1825; died, London, in 1855.

Woodville was educated in Baltimore, planning
for a career in medicine, but in 1845 chose to
become an artist instead. Studied painting at the
Düsseldorf Academy from 1845 to 1846, and then
in Düsseldorf privately with Carl Sohn until about
1851. During this period, he sent several works to
exhibitions in the United States. Several of his
paintings were engraved and sent out by the Art-
Union for its members. From 1851, Woodville lived
primarily in London and Paris. His death in
London in 1855 may have been the result of an
overdose of laudanum. His son, another Richard
Caton Woodville, is known chiefly for his illustrations for the Illustrated London News.

145 *Card Players*, 1845–1846, pencil, $10\frac{1}{2} \times 15$
Lent by Mr. Kurt Versen.

146 *The Fencing Lesson*, 1847–1849, pencil, 10×7
Lent by Mr. William Woodville, VIII,
Washington.

147 *Knight and Scribe*, 1852, pencil, heightened with
white, $7\frac{1}{4} \times 7\frac{7}{8}$
Lent by The Baltimore Museum of Art.

148 *The Welcome Drink*, 1843–1855, pencil, $11 \times 9\frac{1}{2}$
Lent by Mr. Kurt Versen.

149 *Seated Woman*, 1845–1855, pencil and white chalk,
$14\frac{1}{2} \times 10\frac{7}{8}$
Lent by Mr. Kurt Versen.

150 *War News from Mexico*, engraving after Woodville
by Alfred Jones, $23 \times 18\frac{1}{2}$
Lent by the Corcoran Gallery of Art, Washington.

Illustrations

The German Artists

1 Andreas Achenbach *Stormy Seascape* 1850

2 Andreas Achenbach *Mountainous Landscape*

3 Andreas Achenbach *Forest Deep in Snow*

4 Oswald Achenbach *Footbridge over a Stream* 1843

5 Oswald Achenbach *Precipice near Bozen* 1845

6 Oswald Achenbach *Olive Grove near Torbole at Lake Garda* 1845

7 Oswald Achenbach *View from Trier (Mosel)* 1869

9 Eduard J. F. Bendemann *Landscape: Ebermannstadt* 1854

8 Oswald Achenbach *Lazzerone* (*Neapolitan Laborer*)

12 Eduard J. F. Bendemann *Portrait of a Man* 1860

11 Eduard J. F. Bendemann *Wilhelm von Schadow on his Sickbed* 1860

10 Eduard J. F. Bendemann *Portrait of Ludwig Richter* 1858

13 Eduard J. F. Bendemann *Study for a Wall Painting*

14 Eduard J. F. Bendemann *Grape Harvest—Study for a Wall Painting*

15 Christian Eduard Boettcher *Children Returning from Gathering Leaves* 1850

16 Christian Eduard Boettcher
Lovers at the Wall 1853

17 Wilhelm Camphausen *Picnic near Ratingen* 1857

19 Wilhelm Camphausen *A Rest in the Grafenberg Forest* 1867

18 Wilhelm Camphausen *Landscape near a Lake* 1866

20 Wilhelm Camphausen *The Hunt—Tristan Sings his Life Story*

21 Ernst Deger *Study for a Crucifixion*

22　Ernst Deger *Figure and Hand Studies*

23　Jacob F. Dielmann *Study of a Woman*

25 Johann Peter Hasenclever *The Winetasters*

26 Johann Peter Hasenclever *An Artist's Studio*

24 Johann Peter Hasenclever *Munich Beerhall* 1842

27 Johann Peter Hasenclever *A Travelling Company*

Seinem Freunde Gustav Grunbach — Th Hildebrandt.
August 1864.

28 Ferdinand Theodor Hildebrandt *Portrait of a Lady* 1864

29 Rudolf Jordan *The Wedding Procession* 1836

30 Rudolf Jordan *Women Awaiting the Return of the Fishermen* 1852

31 Carl Friedrich Lessing *Mountain Landscape in a Storm* 1825

32 Carl Friedrich Lessing *Study for* "*The Storming of Iconium*" 1831

33 Carl Friedrich Lessing *Walther and Hildegunde* 1834

34 Carl Friedrich Lessing *Crusader's Watch* 1834–1835

35 Carl Friedrich Lessing *Jan Hus before the Council of Constance* 1845

36 Carl Friedrich Lessing *Family Portrait* 1845

37 Carl Friedrich Lessing *The Crusaders Find a Spring in the Desert* 1849

38 Carl Friedrich Lessing *Rocky Landscape in the Harz Mountains: Regenstein* 1852

39 Carl Friedrich Lessing *Hills and Fields: Michelstein* 1852

40 Carl Friedrich Lessing *Near Halberstadt* 1852

41 Carl Friedrich Lessing *Rocky Hill and Forest : Michelstein* 1852

42 Carl Friedrich Lessing *Portrait of Worthington Whittredge* 1853

43 Carl Friedrich Lessing *Tree Study* 1853

44 Carl Friedrich Lessing *Old Man in a Monk's Robe*

45 Carl Friedrich Lessing *The Capture of Pope Paschal II*

46 Heinrich Carl Anton Mücke *St. Hubert* 1836

47 Heinrich Carl Anton Mücke *Hunter and Nymph*

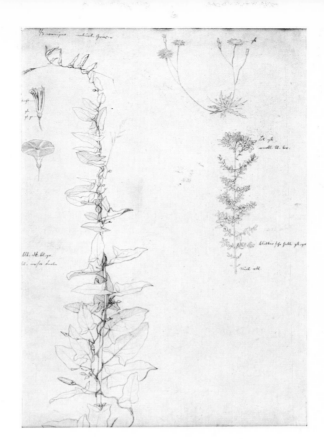

48 Johann Wilhelm Preyer *Studies of Plants* 1833

49 Johann Wilhelm Preyer *Still Life* 1880

51 Alfred Rethel *The Baptism of Widukind*

52 Alfred Rethel *The Destruction of Jerusalem*

50 Alfred Rethel *Study for a Monk with a Cross*

53 Henry Ritter *The Artist's Children* 1846

55 Henry Ritter *In the Studio*

Der letzte der Mohicaner.

54 Henry Ritter *The Last of the Mohicans*

57 Friedrich Wilhelm von Schadow *Floating Figure of a Woman*

58 Friedrich Wilhelm von Schadow *Floating Figure of a Woman*

56 Friedrich Wilhelm von Schadow *Study for a Portrait of Banker Fraenkel's Daughter* 1824–1825

59 Caspar J. N. Scheuren *The Four Seasons: Spring* 1865

60 Caspar J. N. Scheuren *The Four Seasons: Summer* 1865

61 Caspar J. N. Scheuren *The Four Seasons : Autumn* 1865

62 Caspar J. N. Scheuren *The Four Seasons : Winter* 1865

63 Caspar J. N. Scheuren *Ruins on the Rhine*

64 Johann Wilhem Schirmer *View into the Park of the Villa Borghese* 1839–1840

65 Johann Wilhem Schirmer *Cypresses* 1840

66 Johann Wilhelm Schirmer *Hessian Landscape* 1849

67 Johann Wilhelm Schirmer *Landscape with the Flight into Egypt*

68 Johann Wilhelm Schirmer *Forest Landscape with an Aqueduct*

69 Johann Wilhelm Schirmer *Landscape*

70 Adolf Schroedter *The Winetasting* 1850

71 Arnold Schulten *Romantic Landscape with a Castle* 1835

72 Arnold Schulten *Landscape with Worshippers* 1868

75 Johann Baptist Sonderland *The Farewell*

73 Carl Ferdinand Sohn *Two Young Ladies* 1850

74 Johann Baptist Sonderland *The Sermon of Jan Hus* 1835 (drawing after Lessing's painting.)

76 Wilhelm Volkhardt *Head and Hand Studies*

78 J. B. W. August Weber *Landscape*

77 J. B. W. August Weber *Study of a Tree*

The American Artists

79 Albert Bierstadt. A page from the artist's *Sketchbook* 1853

80 Albert Bierstadt *Study Made in Germany* 1853

81 Albert Bierstadt *German Costume Study*
ca. 1853

82 Albert Bierstadt *Study of a Ewe* ca. 1855

83 Albert Bierstadt *Study of Rocks and Trees by a Lake* ca. 1863

84 Albert Bierstadt *Moselkern, Germany* 1864

85 Albert Bierstadt *Rocky Mountains, The Valley of the Yosemite* 1866 (an engraving by James Smillie after the painting by Bierstadt)

86 George Caleb Bingham *Seated Man in a Broad-brimmed Hat* 1836

87 George Caleb Bingham *Man Standing with Pipe* ca. 1857

88 George Caleb Bingham *Pan Player*

89 George Caleb Bingham *Fiddler*

91 George Caleb Bingham *Spectator Seated, Back View*

90 George Caleb Bingham *Man with Pipe, Seated*

92 George Caleb Bingham *Spectator Seated, Front View*

93 James McDougal Hart *Still Life* 1856

94 James McDougal Hart *Trees and Stream* 1861

95 James McDougal Hart *Tree and Picket Fence* 1863

96 James McDougal Hart *Cows Resting* 1871

97 James McDougal Hart *Study of Sheep* 1872

98 James McDougal Hart *Louella* 1879

99 William Stanley Haseltine *Oleavana—Campagna Romana* 1858

100 William Stanley Haseltine *Tivoli* 1858

102 William Stanley Haseltine *Olive Grove at Tivoli*

101 William Stanley Haseltine *Blankenbergh* 1876

103 William Stanley Haseltine *Fishing Boats on a Beach*

104 William Stanley Haseltine *Nahant—Egg Rock*

Langhamer

E. Johnson
Düsseldorf
Nov. 1849.

105 Eastman Johnson *Portrait of Langhamer* 1849

Col. Lottner.

Düsseldorf June. 1850.
E. J.

106 Eastman Johnson *Colonel Lottner* 1850

108 Eastman Johnson *Counterfeiters*, 1854

107 Eastman Johnson *Three Dutch Figures* ca. 1852

109 Eastman Johnson *Study of an Oriental* ca. 1851–1855

110 Eastman Johnson *Polly Gary* 1855

112 Eastman Johnson *Old Woman and Child* ca. 1860

111 Eastman Johnson *Secretary Dobbins* 1856

114 Eastman Johnson *Captain Myrick* 1880

113 Eastman Johnson *Husking* 1875

116 Eastman Johnson *Berry Picking*

115 Eastman Johnson *Richard Peters*

117 Emanuel Gottlieb Leutze *Cathedral Ruins* ca. 1845

118 Emanuel Gottlieb Leutze *Study of Eastman Johnson* 1850

119 Emanuel Gottlieb Leutze *Preaching to the Indians* 1852

120 Emanuel Gottlieb Leutze *David Playing before Saul* 1853

121 Emanuel Gottlieb Leutze *The Soldier's Farewell* 1859

122 Emanuel Gottlieb Leutze *Study for "Westward the Course of Empire Takes its Way,"* ca. 1860

123 Emanuel Gottlieb Leutze *Seventh Regiment, Camp Cameron, Stacked Rifles* 1861

125 Emanuel Gottlieb Leutze *Studies with Washington's Head*

124 Emanuel Gottlieb Leutze *Gold Mining, Central City* 1861

126 Emanuel Gottlieb Leutze *Leutze, Painting*
(*Self-Caricature*)

127 Emanuel Gottlieb Leutze *The Dear Lumpish Baby*

128 Emanuel Gottlieb Leutze *Landscape in Thundershower*

129 Emanuel Gottlieb Leutze *Hind Quarters of a Horse*

130 Emanuel Gottlieb Leutze *Head of a Girl in a Hat*

131 Emanuel Gottlieb Leutze *The Last Drop*

132 William Trost Richards *Woods* 1865

133 William Trost Richards *Grindelwald, Switzerland* 1867

134 William Trost Richards *Franconia Mountains from Compton, New Hampshire* 1872

135 William Trost Richards *Baldart Castle* 1892

136 William Trost Richards *East Hampton Beach*

137 Worthington Whittredge *Sketch from Nature* 1853

138 Worthington Whittredge *Study of Three Boats* 1856

Le Bulle Isole
Sept. 15. 1857

139 Worthington Whittredge *Isola dei Pescatori, Lago Maggiore* 1857

140 Worthington Whittredge *View of Lake and Houses* ca. 1857

141 Worthington Whittredge
Study of a Tree 1871

142 Worthington Whittredge *Bishop Berkeley's House, Newport, Rhode Island* 1877

143 Worthington Whittredge *Hillside, Group of Figures Outside a Row of Houses*

144 Worthington Whittredge *Sketch from "Crossing the Ford, Platte River, Colorado"*

145 Richard Caton Woodville *Card Players* 1845–1846

146 Richard Caton Woodville *The Fencing Lesson* 1847–1849

147 Richard Caton Woodville *Knight and Scribe* 1852

148 Richard Caton Woodville *The Welcome Drink* 1843–1855

149 Richard Caton Woodville *Seated Woman* 1845–1855

150 Richard Caton Woodville *War News from Mexico* (engraving after Woodville's painting by Alfred Jones)

Selected Bibliography

Baur, J. I. H., ed., *The Autobiography of Worthington Whittredge*, Brooklyn Institute of Arts and Sciences, 1942.

Born, Wolfgang, *American Landscape Painting, An Interpretation*, New Haven, Conn., 1948.

Bulletin of the American Art-Union, New York, 1849–1851.

Catalogue of a Private Collection of Paintings and Original Drawings by Artists of the Düsseldorf Academy of Fine Arts, New York, 1851.

Charles Wimar, Introduction by P. S. Rathbone, City Art Museum of St. Louis, 1946.

Die Düsseldorfer Malerschule, Kataloge des Kunstmuseums Düsseldorf, Introduction by I. Markowitz, Kunstmuseum, Düsseldorf, 1969.

Drawings by Carl Friedrich Lessing, Introduction by V. Leuschner, Cincinnati Art Museum, 1972.

Durand, J., and Stillman, W. J., eds., *The Crayon*, Vols. I-VIII, (January 1855–July 1861), New York.

Flexner, James Thomas, *That Wilder Image, The Painting of America's Native School from Thomas Cole to Winslow Homer*, Boston and Toronto, 1962.

German Painting of the 19th Century, Introduction by K. S. Champa and K. H. Champa, Yale University Art Gallery, New Haven, 1970.

Handzeichnungen und Aquarelle, 1800–1850: Bildhefte des Kunstmuseums Düsseldorf, Introduction by D. Graf, Düsseldorf, 1971.

Hendricks, G., *Albert Bierstadt*, Amon Carter Museum, Fort Worth, Texas, 1972.

Hills, Patricia, *Eastman Johnson*, Whitney Museum of American Art, New York, 1972.

Howat, John K., "Washington Crossing the Delaware," *The Metropolitan Museum of Art Bulletin*, Vol. XXVI, No. 7 (March, 1968)

Hutt, Wolfgang, *Die Düsseldorfer Malerschule 1819–1869*, Leipzig, 1964.

M. and M. Karolik Collection of American Watercolors and Drawings, 1800–1875, Vol. I, Introduction by H. P. Rossiter, Museum of Fine Arts, Boston, 1962.

Novotny, Fritz, *Painting and Sculpture in Europe, 1780–1880*, Baltimore, Maryland, 1960.

Pevsner, Nicholas, *Academics of Art, Past and Present*, Cambridge, Massachusetts, 1940.

Plowden, Helen H., *William Stanley Haseltine, Sea and Landscape Painter*, London, 1947.

Richard Caton Woodville, an Early American Genre Painter, Introduction by F. S. Grubar, The Corcoran Gallery of Art, Washington, D.C., 1967.

Scheyer, Ernst, "Leutze und Lessing, Amerika und Düsseldorf," *Aurora/Eichendorf Almanach*, Regensburg, 1966.

Stehle, Raymond L., "Five Sketchbooks of Emanuel Leutze," *The Quarterly Journal of the Library of Congress*, Vol. 21, No. 2 (April, 1964).

Triumph of Realism, Introduction by A. von Saldern, The Brooklyn Museum, 1967.

Worthington Whittredge, A Retrospective Exhibition of an American Artist, Introduction by E. H. Dwight, Munson-Williams-Proctor Institute, Utica, New York, 1969.